Reasons and Rationalizations:

The Limits to Organizational Knowledge

CHRIS ARGYRIS

OXFORD
UNIVERSITY PRESS

OXFORD

UNIVERSITY PRESS

Great Clarendon Street, Oxford OX2 6DP

Oxford University press is a department of the University of Oxford.
It furthers the University's objective of excellence in research, scholarship,
and education by publishing worldwide in

Oxford New York

Auckland Cape Town Dar es Salaam Hong Kong Karachi
Kuala Lumpur Madrid Melbourne Mexico City Nairobi
New Delhi Shanghai Taipei Toronto

With offices in

Argentina Austria Brazil Chile Czech Republic France Greece
Guatemala Hungary Italy Japan Poland Portugal Singapore
South Korea Switzerland Thailand Turkey Ukraine Vietnam

Oxford is a registered trade mark of Oxford University Press
in the UK and in certain other countries

Published in the United States
by Oxford University Press Inc., New York

British Library Cataloguing in Publication Date
Data available

Library of Congress Cataloging in Publication Data
Data available

Typeset by Newgen Imaging Systems (P) Ltd., Chennai, India
Printed in Great Britain
on acid-free paper by
CPI Bath

ISBN 0–19–926807–X   978–0–19–926807–8
ISBN 0–19–928682–5 (Pbk.)   978–0–19–928682–9 (Pbk.)

1 3 5 7 9 10 8 6 4 2

PREFACE

Early in my career, I made two choices: first, to design and help implement liberating alternatives for human beings and organizations; and second, to do so through scholarly inquiry and research.

I begin this book by citing the literature that documents executives' *and* employees' use of defensive reasoning mind-sets that practically assure that the liberating alternatives they espouse will not be implemented. When the practitioners are pressed as to why they act in ways that are counterproductive to their intentions and goals, they claim that they are victims, helpless in the face of the demands of others and of organizations. These are not conditions favorable to the non-trivial changes that are required to produce liberating alternatives.

Turning to scholarly research on organizations, we have a puzzle. It is the scholars who document the practitioners' defensive reasoning mind-sets and organizational defensive routines. It is the scholars who show that these features have a counterproductive effect on human beings and organization. The puzzle is that these same scholars do not conduct research designed to mitigate these counterproductive consequences. Why?

The scholars' typical answers are, I suggest, incomplete and may be misleading. I hope to show that we as scholars have our own defensive reasoning mind-sets and that the scholarly communities that we create are full of defensive routines. The most powerful defenses, I will suggest, are the ideas in good currency about theory creation and research methodologies.

→ Scholars and practitioners are victims of their own defensive policies and practices. Scholars and practitioners appear to create a situation of the blind leading the blind.

I end the book by defining a perspective and providing several that illustrate some ways to begin to solve the puzzle. Neither the perspective nor the illustrations are as powerful as is required. They are, I hope, a valid beginning.

I should like to thank Dianne Argyris and Alan Kantrow for their helpful comments. Catherine Van Arnam was indispensable in producing the manuscript.

Chris Argyris
March 2003

CONTENTS

1

Introduction

In order to act, human beings diagnose problems, invent solutions, produce the solutions, and evaluate the effectiveness of what they have produced. I should like to define mind-set as the reasoning processes human beings use to test the validity and effectiveness of these actions. A mind-set tells the actors how they are making sense of the world in which they exist *and* the validity of their sense-making processes.

THE DEFENSIVE REASONING MIND-SET

The characteristics of a defensive reasoning mind-set include the following:

1. The objective is to protect and defend actor(s) or supra-individual unities such as groups, inter-groups, and organizations.
2. The primary reasoning processes include making the premises explicit (on the assumption that they are valid) and testing them by the use of self-referential logic. Self-referential logic means testing a claim by the same logic that generated it in the first place. For example, the claim 'trust me, I know this organization' should be tested by the same reasoning that the person making the claim is using.
3. Transparency is avoided in the service of protecting the self and denying that one is protecting the self.

4. Self-deception is denied by cover-up. In order for the cover-up to work, it too must be covered up.

The consequences of defensive reasoning include escalating misunderstanding, self-fulfilling prophecies, and self-sealing processes. All these escalate because the logic used is self-referential, which does not encourage the detection and correction of error.

When these conditions are combined, a generic syndrome against learning is created. This in turn leads human beings to doubt that errors are unlikely to be genuinely corrected. These doubts and the conditions described above combine to create a sense of helplessness and a stance of being a victim, both of which lead to adaptation strategies that help to ensure that defensive consequences will persist.

Defensive reasoning thrives in contexts where the defensive features cannot be legitimately challenged. One consequence of this is that not only are issues undiscussable, but that undiscussability is itself undiscussable, so that such generic rules as cover-up, and cover-up of the original cover-up, lack transparency.

Conditions such as these make the world of defensive reasoning primarily an underground organization. Its existence is known, but actions are rarely taken to correct its counterproductive effects, mainly because, as we shall see, those who share the defensive reasoning mind-set believe that they must continue doing so to prevent the organization from going out of control, from imploding. Organizational defenses, they claim, are necessary to protect organizations from their own defenses. This results in ultra-stable systems that are self-sealing and anti-corrective. Human beings report that they are helpless to make any changes because they do not know what to do, and because, as victims, they could not act to reverse the ultra-stable anti-learning state of their universe.

I should like to focus upon the compulsive repetition of errors—the apparent lack of corrective learning, even though the practitioners acknowledge its counterproductive effect on performance. Why do people create the very conditions they abhor? Why do they compulsively repeat errors? One answer is that the very use of the defensive reasoning mind-set and of organizational defenses causes them to do so. Such an explanation is circular. It is valid because circularity is a key feature of such phenomena. The question remains: why and by what processes are these circularities created in the first place?

THE PRODUCTIVE REASONING MIND-SET

People who use defensive reasoning mind-sets also use productive reasoning mind-sets.

Productive reasoning (1) produces valid and validatable knowledge, (2) creates informed choices, and (3) makes personal reasoning transparent in order for the claims to be tested robustly. The core of productive reasoning is that the parties involved are vigilant about striving to avoid unknowingly deceiving themselves and others. The managerial disciplines used to design and manage organizations are dedicated to the increasing use of productive reasoning (Jensen, 2000).

But then, why do individuals not use productive reasoning in dealing with such problems as defensive routines and the defensive reasoning mind-set? Some practitioners, and indeed some scholars (as we shall see), claim that this is never likely to occur.

ORGANIZATIONAL INNER CONTRADICTIONS

The coexistence of productive reasoning and defensive reasoning produces inner contradictions. Successful productive reasoning requires the existence of defensive reasoning. The second feature of this inner contradiction, as we shall see, is that, as the transparent above-ground organizational world is strengthened, the underground world is also strengthened.

However, the underground bubble may be pierced by any crisis that brings the underground world to the surface, whether the participants like it or not. Examples include the Enron–Arthur Andersen fiasco, the lack of cooperation between the FBI and the CIA, and the tragedy of the Challenger flight (Argyris 1990*a*). The cover-up of questionable and, at times, illegal actions by the Catholic hierarchy is another example. The press has reported cases of teachers giving pupils the correct answers to test questions so that the schools can obtain higher evaluations. In all these cases, the participants blame others or the system. They were the victims. They were helpless and they had to cover up.

Parker (2002) provides illustrations of management and employees colluding to violate rules of practice and to conceal their actions. Reading her review, I was reminded of the following recent personal experience with a corporation in Europe. During a 'break-out' session a shop steward described a practice of assigning employees to work overtime on Saturdays in order to produce a certain product. Local management and the workers knew that the product was not needed. They warehoused it in an abandoned area in the plant.

Not surprisingly, these self-fueling processes are difficult to interrupt. Whistle-blowers are required to expose them, but, by doing so, they violate the protective games of the underground system. They are therefore often characterized as immature trouble-makers.

A recent article in the *Wall Street Journal* (2002) identifies an even more pernicious problem. For several decades, 3M has been described as a model innovative organization. The article quotes the new CEO as finding an organization that lacked most of the features that made organizations great. The CEO maintains that the staff were capable of being innovative, but the organization deteriorated because its defensive routines remained hidden below the surface. Mills (2002), in explaining the Enron-Arthur Andersen debacle, argues that accounting has changed subtly but significantly over the years. It has moved from providing proper information to providing accounting interpretations that are favorable to the client.

The question arises: what were the features of 3M, or the accounting profession as an institution, that kept the subtle changes underground? What kind of knowledge would be required to prevent this long-run cover-up? Answers to these questions might lead to fewer executives doing things like voting Enron, as they did, one of the best-managed companies, noted for its excellent human resources policies supporting openness and honesty (Salter 2003).

How is it that the underground world remains so robustly when it stands in opposition to the above-ground world? How is it that human beings develop the skills of defensive reasoning? To my knowledge, neither educational programs in universities nor company programs are dedicated to helping individuals and organizations become skilled at defensive reasoning. They don't recommend or teach the skills required to produce organizational anti-learning practices such as skilled incompetence, skilled unawareness, and organizational defensive routines. Yet the core features of the defensive reasoning mind-set are omnipresent and powerful. Where and how are the ideas and the skills taught? Why are they maintained even though they inhibit the implementation of productive reasoning and its positive consequences for organizations?

THE DEFENSIVE REASONING MIND-SET IN THE CONDUCT OF ORGANIZATIONAL RESEARCH

Scholars, I hope to show, also use a defensive reasoning mind-set, especially when they conduct research on how organizations deal with difficult, 'wicked' problems that threaten existing routines and the status quo. One reason for the inconsistencies produced by practitioners with their apparent systematic blindness may be that the scholars who document these problems do not conduct research on how to overcome them.

Why do scholars systematically neglect or bypass the challenge of reducing the defensive reasoning mind-set of practitioners? If this claim is true, does it not violate the fundamental value of scholarly research, namely, the vigilant quest to expand knowledge about problems, especially those that it identifies as important?

I hope to show that there are fundamental structural causes for these inconsistencies. They are structural in the sense that they are caused by the fundamental norms and rules scholars use when they conduct research. For example, scholars assert that their fundamental purpose is to describe their chosen universe as completely and validly as possible. I hope to show that the dedication to the description of the universe 'as is' makes it unlikely that scholars will conduct studies about how the universe 'as is' reacts when its fundamental features are questioned. In order for such research to be conducted, it is necessary to introduce the concept of a new or rare universe, to produce it empirically, and to specify how to move from here to there.

In order to produce the new universe, 'subjects' are needed who have the skills to do so. But if they had such skills, they would be part of the existing universe. Moreover, it would be necessary to have norms that sanction and encourage the new behavior. Again, if these existed, it would mean they were part of the organizational universe 'as is'.

Scholars have the skills to describe universes that exist. They are not taught the skills to create new universes. Moreover, they often lack the power necessary to product such new universes. In order to create the new universes they require the assistance of people with power in the present universe who are willing to take the necessary risks. But it is unlikely that such individuals would take such risks with scholars who themselves do not have the requisite skills.

Why do scholars not have the requisite skills? Indeed, why do practitioners not have the requisite skills? The answer, I will suggest, is that most human beings are acculturated early in life, long before they become scholars or executives, to use a defensive reasoning mind-set when dealing with the challenge of handling difficult, 'wicked' problems and changing the status quo. Moreover, they create organizational and community defensive routines to support their continued use of defensive reasoning.

In the case of executives, they sanction all sorts of programs on leadership, learning, change, and commitment, that espouse changing the status quo but actually maintain it (Argyris 2000). In the case of scholars, they espouse the dedicated search for truth, yet they create community rules and norms that inhibit such inquiry when the issues are about fundamental changes of the universe they have chosen to study (Chapter 5).

The source of these claims is a theory and research called a Theory of Action.

A BRIEF OUTLINE OF A THEORY OF ACTION

Effective action[1] is the fundamental objective of human and organizational performance. Action is effective to the extent that it is consistent with intention, that it persists, and that it does so without harming the existing level of organizational performance.

Learning at any level is about producing action that approximates as closely as possible to the three criteria just identified. Learning from this perspective requires the creation of new knowledge, new insights, and new understandings, but goes further. Learning occurs when these three features are all in the service of effective action. How do we know when we have learned something? The answer is: when we can produce what we claim we have learned.

Action is produced by the activation of procedural knowledge stored in our heads (or minds or brains). Procedural knowledge informs us how to design actions that can be implemented. Procedural knowledge depends upon causality. Causality embedded in procedural knowledge specifies the consequences that are achieved. As Van der Heijden *et al.* (2002: 153) write, 'The assumption of causality is one of the most fundamental structural features the human mind imposes on reality in order to make sense of it'.

---

[1] For a different perspective on increasing the value of social science, see Anderson, Herriot, and Hodgkinson (2001) and Flyvbjerg (2001).

It is not possible for human beings to engage *de novo* the full complexity of the environment in which they exist. Life would pass them by. Human beings deal with the challenge by constructing theories of action that they can use to act in concrete situations. Such theories of action are master designs that specify the actions and their causal sequencing required in order to act effectively; and they are normative because effectiveness is a concept of personal or societal choice.

Theories of action are of two types. One is the theory that we espouse, which is composed of values, beliefs, and action strategies. The other is the theory-in-use, which is stored in our heads in the form of designs that are composed of action strategies, intended consequences organized in causal sequence. We call these designs-in-use. Our designs-in-use, when combined, constitute our theory-in-use. The theory-in-use is the master program; designs-in-use are sub-routines.

This perspective about effective actions (discussed in more detail in Chapter 8) is consistent with folk or design theory as exemplified by Simon (1969) and the connectionist perspective as described by Churchland (2000). Some scholars describe the Simon perspective as bottom-up and the Churchland perspective as top-down. So far in my work I have found the former, designs-in-use perspective more helpful. It is this perspective that has helped me to understand and to educate human beings in double-loop learning. As is frequently the case, we will eventually find how these perspectives can be integrated.

The Theory of Action approach, developed by myself and Donald Schön, is founded upon the importance of programs stored in our heads that are activated by human beings as they are needed. We have developed this perspective in several publications (Argyris 1982; 1990a; 1993; Argyris, Putnam, and Smith 1985; Argyris and Schön 1974; 1996). I will summarize a few of the more important claims that are relevant to single and double-loop learning and implementable validity (see also Chapter 8).

The theory-in-use is called Model I. A Model I theory-in-use is composed of the governing variables or values. They are: (1) be in unilateral control over others, (2) strive to win and minimize losing, (3) suppress negative feelings, and (4) act rationally, which, as we shall see, means using defensive reasoning. The three dominant action strategies are to advocate one's position, to evaluate the actions of others and oneself, and to make attributions about others' and one's own intentions. These action strategies are crafted so as to minimize any encouragement of inquiry and testing. The most important consequences of Model I theory-in-use include misunderstanding, escalating errors, self-sealing processes, and self-fulfilling, counterproductive, self-fueling processes.

Model I theory-in-use is used regardless of age, gender, race, wealth, education, type of organization, and culture. The theory-in-use does not vary but actions may vary. Actions, however, do not vary in ways that are inconsistent with Model I. For example, human beings using Model I strive to minimize the possibility of being held responsible for making others defensive. In Britain such actions may be called 'being civilized', in America, 'being diplomatic', in the Far East 'being thoughtful and polite'. They are all implemented with values and action strategies consistent with Model I values.

Human beings programmed with Model I theory-in-use create behavioral worlds in organizations that are consistent with Model I. One of the most powerful features is organizational defensive routines. (Some recent illustrations can be found in Charan and Useem 2002, and in Nutt 2002. See also Chapters 2, 3, and 4.) An organizational defensive routine is any policy, practice, or action that prevents embarrassment or threat, but does so in ways that prevent discovery of the cause of the embarrassment or threat. Organizational defensive routines inhibit learning, especially double-loop learning.

An example is organizational mixed messages. 'Mary, you are in charge, but check with Charles.' 'Bill, be creative, but be careful.'

The theory-in-use to produce mixed messages includes the following rules:

1. Communicate a message that is mixed.
2. Act as if it is not mixed.
3. Make A and B undiscussable.
4. Act as if you are not doing any of the above.

DOUBLE-LOOP LEARNING

Double-loop learning is the detection and correction of errors where the correction requires changes not only in action strategies but also in the values that govern the theory-in-use. Double-loop learning questions the status quo and encourages rare events. Single-loop learning is the detection and correction of errors that does not require changing the values that govern the existing theory-in-use, in our case Model I and organizational defensive routines. A thermostat is a single-loop learner. It is programmed to increase or decrease the heat in order to keep the temperature constant. A thermostat could be a double-loop learner if it inquired why it should measure heat and why it is set so that the temperature is constant.

Changing organizational defensive routines that inhibit learning and cover-up require double-loop learning, because the Model I theories-in-use would have to be altered. A theory-in-use that may be used to produce double-loop learning is Model II. The governing values are: (1) producing valid information, (2) informed choice, and (3) vigilant monitoring of the effectiveness of the implemented actions to assess its degree of effectiveness.

Model II is not the opposite of Model I. The governing values of the opposite of Model I would be: (1) everyone is in control, (2) everyone wins, (3) feelings are expressed, (4) rationality is downplayed. These were the governing values of the early 'T group' laboratories and leadership education, which did not enhance double-loop learning even though that was the intention (Argyris 1982).

The action strategies of Model II also advocate a position, making evaluations and attributions. The difference is that these action strategies are now in the service of the governing values of Model II rather than Model I. This means that the emphasis is upon inquiry and testing.

Asking human beings to alter their theory-in-use is asking them to question the foundation of their sense of competence and self-confidence related to producing effective action. It is also

asking them to design and implement organizations that do not
encourage competitive infighting, unilateral control, and commitment to the dictates of organizational defensive routines.

This is a tall order but we are learning that it is doable. First, the
solution is not to eliminate Model I, but to use it where such skills
make sense (for example, dealing with routine issues). Second, the
intention is to provide human beings with two degrees of freedom
to choose Models I and II where appropriate. Third, another solution is to create organizational structures and policies that encourage the use of double-loop learning in managing performance
(Chapters 6 and 7).

Double-loop learning, in a world dominated by Model I and
organizational defensive routines, is not a recipe for 'positive', 'feel-
good', 'politically correct' action. It requires, therefore, not only
changes in theory-in-use but also changes in the organizational-
cultural context involved.

Theories-in-use, be they Model I or Model II, are generated as
human beings learn to act skillfully and consistently with their
requirements. The necessity to be skillful in order to create the
designs-in-use generates a puzzle. Model I produces actions that
are skillful yet incompetent because they produce consequences
that the actors do not intend. The actors are unaware of their skillful incompetence while producing it.

The puzzle is this. If skillful incompetence is produced by a
match with Model I, then it is not an error. If unawareness is skillful then it must be produced by some design-in-use. Skillful
unawareness is therefore also a match with some design-in-use.

How come human beings are skillfully incompetent and
unaware? One answer is that the very action required to become
skillful produces unawareness. Once human beings become skilled,
they forget much of what they went through to become skillful.
Skillful actions are those that 'work', that appear effortless, that
are automatic and usually tacit, and that are taken for granted.
A consequence of generating skills is designed ignorance.

The second reason for skilled incompetence and skilled
unawareness is that Model I organizational defensive behavioral

systems encourage cover-up. In order for a cover-up to be effective, the intention must also be covered up. It is unlikely that human beings will give or receive useful feedback to deal with their skilled incompetence and skilled unawareness. (Illustrations will be given throughout the book, especially in Chapters 6 and 7.)

The defensive reasoning mind-set is created and maintained by human beings using Model I theories-in-use and by organizational defensive routines at all levels of the organization. The productive reasoning mind-set is created and maintained by human beings using Model II theories-in-use and by organizational norms that encourage good dialectic and effective communication.

Strengthening the productive mind-set and, at the same time, reducing the defensive reasoning mind-set requires double-loop learning. This book focuses on an important puzzle. As we shall see, defensive reasoning and counterproductive defensive norms are widely reported by scholars. Yet the scholars cited do not conduct research on how to overcome the selfsame defensive features that they identify. Why is it that scholarship in organizations seems to stop with describing these features and does not continue with research to change them?

One answer, as we shall see, is that scholars do not respect implementable validity as they do internal and external validity (see Chapter 5). Many of the ideas in good currency in normal science or humanistic interpretive research do not reward studies that attempt to *create* (not simply understand) double-loop learning in organizations in such ways that learning is effective and persistent (Chapter 5).

IMPLEMENTABLE VALIDITY

The effectiveness of implementing actions increases as:

- the validity of the models used to diagnose and to solve problems increases;
- the actors intend to implement the models;
- the actors have the skills to implement the models; and

- the context in which the implementation occurs is supportive of implementing the actions.

The model just stated applies to all types of implementation. It is useful, however, to distinguish between internal and external implementation. Internal implementation means implementing the model
correctly so that the predicted consequences ensue. For example,
human beings may strive to develop strategies for competitiveness
by using concepts such as Five Forces (Porter 1980) or concepts
that are used to develop core competencies (Drejer 2002). Internal
implementation refers to developing these strategies and producing
recommendations to enhance organizational competitiveness.

External implementation means the actions taken to implement the recommendations throughout the organization. Here
the model is about generating acceptance of, and internal commitment to, implementing the recommendations. Ideally, each of
these orientations should affect the other. Unfortunately, there is
little research that illustrates how this can be done (some examples
are presented in Chapter 7). Until more research into external
implementation is produced, we will be left with research that
offers advice about effective external implementation but does not
provide prescriptive knowledge about how to produce it.

For example, Krogh, Ichijo, and Nonaka (2002) advise that caring can be at the heart of a good discussion that has many consequences related to managerial disciplines. The difficulties arise
when individuals use Model I theories- in-use to assist in producing consequences related to managerial disciplines. The defensive
reasoning that underlies the former conflicts with productive reasoning. To compound the difficulty, individuals use Model I
actions to produce Model I caring that is quite different from the
Model II actions that genuine caring requires. Box 1.1 illustrates
these differences around such virtues as caring, help, support,
respect, strength, honesty, and integrity.

Throughout the book, and especially in Chapters 6 and 7, we
will find many examples where the participants act consistently
with Model I caring (and the other social virtues) yet expect the
consequences that are produced by Model II actions (Box 1.1). One

Box 1.1. Model I and Model II social virtues

Model I social virtues	Model II social virtues
Caring, help, and support	
Give approval and praise to other people. Tell others what you believe will make them feel good about themselves. Reduce their feelings of hurt by telling them how much you care and, if possible, agree with them that others acted improperly.	Increase the others' capacity to confront their own ideas, to create a window into their own mind, and to face their unsurfaced assumptions, biases, and fears by acting in these ways toward other people.
Respect for others	
Defer to other people and do not confront their reasoning or actions.	Attribute to other people a high capacity for self-reflection and self-examination without becoming so upset that they lose their effectiveness and their sense of self-responsibility and choice. Keep testing this attribution (openly).
Strength	
Advocate your position in order to win. Hold your own position in the face of advocacy. Feeling vulnerable is a sign of weakness.	Advocate your position and combine it with inquiry and self-reflection. Feeling vulnerable while encouraging inquiry is a sign of strength.

Box 1.1. (*Continued*)

Honesty

Tell other people no lies or tell others all you think and feel.	Encourage yourself and other people to say what they know yet fear to say. Minimize what would otherwise be subject to distortion and cover-up of the distortion.

Integrity

Stick to your principles, values, and beliefs.	Advocate your principles, values, and beliefs in a way that invites inquiry into them and encourages other people to do the same.

of the early tasks in educating individuals about this dilemma is to help them to assess the degree to which it is valid for them, the defensive reasoning and actions that keep them from being aware, and the ways in which organizational defensive routines support the modes of reasoning that inhibit double-loop learning. In Chapter 7, illustrations are presented to show that this learning can be produced.

In this book (and in previous publications cited above) numerous examples are presented that show that the inner contradictions, gaps, and inconsistencies of research findings do not surface until attempts are made to implement them. This is especially true of double-loop issues. Implementable validity, I suggest, needs to be elevated to the same status as internal and external validity if we are to provide human beings with actionable knowledge about effective action.

Without research that focuses on double-loop learning and implementable validity, we are likely to retain and reinforce the defensive reasoning mind-set. As Dror (2002) shows, although the limitations of governance have been documented for many decades, there is little discernible progress in correcting them. Indeed, Dror suggests that we are moving toward a dead end, then presents suggestions about improving governance. He does not inquire, however, into the defensive mind-set and routines that prevented progress in the past. These features are likely to persist and to be instrumental in inhibiting the implementation of his recommendations. Dror suggests that the often-made characterization of some domain of activity as 'ungovernable' is a defense that should not be tolerated. What is needed is research that produces valid propositions, specifying how to expose and reduce such defensive mind-sets.

THE ARGUMENT OF THIS BOOK

1. Documentation is presented in Chapters 2, 3, and 4 showing that organizations contain powerful defensive routines. The scholars explain the omnipresence of these organization-wide defensive routines as 'natural' to organizations. The same research leads practitioners and scholars to conclude that defensive routines exist in patterns that are so tightly knit that attempts to reduce or remove them could be dangerous and risky to the organization as a whole.

2. Scholars conduct little research on how to reduce the organization-wide defensive routines that they document. They thus violate one of the most fundamental norms of scholarly inquiry, namely, the unrelenting quest to expand valid knowledge about organizations. Scholars explain the self-imposed limits as being consistent with the rules and norms of their community of practice. They consider actions that ignore or violate these rules and norms as dangerous and risky to the generation of valid knowledge and to their careers.

3. Such reasoning by practitioners and scholars is defensive and self-protective. The claim by practitioners that striving to change the defensive routines is dangerous and risky is self-serving in that

it places defensive routines out of bounds. The claim by scholars that conducting double-loop research is dangerous and risky because it violates the rules and norms of scholarly communities is also self-serving.

Both claims are consistent with a defensive reasoning mind-set. For example, if scholars were to confront their defensive reasoning mind-set, they would find that they would have to confront rules and norms that encourage single-loop research and discourage double-loop research. They would also find that the emphasis upon internal and external validity is necessary but not sufficient. Robust tests of validity require the testing of the implementable validity of the knowledge being produced (Chapter 5).

4. Changing the defensive reasoning mind-sets in the management of organizations and in the management of research is a classic example of double-loop learning. The primary reason that practitioners and scholars revert to defensive reasoning, even when their respective theories condemn it, is that they use Model I theory-in-use to solve double-loop problems. Model I theory-in-use is founded on a defensive reasoning mind-set.

In Chapters 6 and 7, an admittedly primitive set of examples is presented on how double-loop research can be conducted. Chapter 8 contains some closing comments.

2

The Corrosion of Character:
Capitalist and Socialist Economics

One of the age-old challenges that organizations face is how to induce human beings to act as responsible agents for creating and maintaining effective organizational performance. The fundamental assumption is that it is management's responsibility to design structures and policies that, when carried out correctly, will lead to effective performance.

Historically speaking, the dominant strategy has been that management decides what the designs should be and how they are to be implemented by the employees in order to be loyal to the organization's requirements and to respect its aspiration for effective performance. Management is assumed to win the employees' commitment through rewards and penalties: by asking them to perform achievable tasks, to obey the management, and to be fairly compensated for doing so. The basis for all this is external commitment: managers induce and employees produce.

The problem in this logic began to appear early in the history of organizations, when management decided to base effective performance upon the division of labor. Some division was necessary because human beings had limited skills and were limited information-processing systems. The problem arose when the tasks were designed to be as simple as possible. The logic was that 'molecularized' tasks were easy to perform, required little training, could be easily managed because of their transparency, and helped to guarantee the easy availability of employees from the labor market. So one reason for the division of labor was economic.

Another reason was that human beings were finite information-processing systems, and were therefore necessarily limited in their capacity to perform. This explains why the division of labor also flourished in non-profit organizations.

The notion of human finiteness made it necessary to limit the number of employees that could be supervised by any one individual. But as the number of supervisors increased, it became necessary to supervise the supervisors in order to monitor their effectiveness. This was the birth of hierarchy. The consequence of the hierarchy was to place employees at every level in a dependent and submissive relationship to those above them. Unilateral control became the hallmark of hierarchy.

Managers saw little reason to be concerned about the hierarchy. They believed that human beings could be required to become the servants in the game of management. They held a view of human beings that Wrong (1961) described as 'over-socialized': human beings are over-socialized when they will willingly conform to legitimate demands of structure. This view did not take into account the potential for human beings to resist being submissive and dependent and required to take on jobs that used only a few of their abilities and their more superficial ones. This created conflict. Individuals in industrialized countries, were increasingly educated and developed to have many abilities, and to seek to outgrow submission and dependence. The conflict was not universal because some adults preferred infantile jobs. However, the majority did not (Argyris 1957).

The result was that individuals began to fight back to reduce the unilateral control and molecularization of their jobs; for example, employees resisted by creating informal activities. However, these solutions were limited. Soon employees created unions to help increase their power over management, and also petitioned their Congressional representatives to produce laws to assure their newfound as well as their future gains.

Management fought back because it saw these employee gains as undermining managerial authority and control. The result was escalating conflict and increasing rigidity on both sides. As competitiveness increased within and between nations (global competition), the defensive rigidities began to be seen by management as counterproductive, since the transaction costs were too high. Sennett (1998) points out that, as the volatility of consumer demand began to increase, organizations and structures of production needed to become more flexible. Flexible specialization became necessary in the modern age because survival and success depended upon getting more varied products ever more quickly to market. This form of production requires employees to make quick decisions, work in small groups, and take risks. 'The most strongly flavored ingredient in this new productive process is the willingness to let the shifting demands of the outside world determine the inside structure of institutions' (Sennett 1998: 52). The old pyramidal structure was too slow to respond.

CORROSION OF CHARACTER IN CAPITALIST COUNTRIES

Flexibility became the hallmark of the new capitalism. According to Sennett, flexibility was produced by both 'discontinuous reinvention of institutions' and 'concentration without centralization'. Examples of the former process included programs for de-layering, re-engineering, downsizing, group participation, and empowerment. Examples of the latter were the use of information technology to instantaneously collect details about the performance of employees, thereby concentrating control yet manufacturing decentralization. Sennett claims that the intention of these programs was to achieve, in a subtle manner, the concentration of control in the hands of top management: so the managerial claim that flexible organizations decentralized power was false.

I reviewed many of the types of programs that Sennett identified (Argyris 2000). I found them to be fads and shams. As I read

Sennett, he believes that management knew these programs were designed to be subtly manipulative in order to maintain the central control that the selfsame programs disavowed. My interpretation is different: the programs were manipulative but the designers did not think they were. Many executives genuinely believed these programs would lead to a new flexible capitalism. The designers of the programs based their thinking and actions upon Model I theory-in-use. They were skillfully incompetent (producing programs that were counterproductive to their intentions) and skillfully unaware of their incompetence.

Take, for example, three internationally known and respected CEOs discussing their views of empowerment (Garvin 1995: 83):

PAUL ALLAIRE (CEO OF XEROX): After all, if you have processes that are in control, you know how the organization is working. There's no guesswork because variances are small and operating limits are well defined. You get quality output without a lot of checking. [And later] You don't need the old command-and-control approach, which was designated to keep people in line; instead, you can tell people to do their own things provided they respect the process. You wind up with an environment that frees people to be creative.

CRAIG WEATHERUP (CEO AND PRESIDENT OF PEPSI-COLA NORTH AMERICA): I agree with you one thousand percent. A process approach *is* [emphasis is speaker's] liberating. It helps us build reliability and winning consistency, and our people love to win. So over time, they've bought in completely.

JAN LESCHLY (CEO OF SMITHKLINE BEECHAM): Sometimes you get the same results by changing the players...it was a gradual process. [And later] People have a tough time understanding what it means for processes to be reliable, repeatable, and in control...and it will take up years before we can honestly say that all 50,000 people at SmithKline Beecham understand what it means to standardize and improve a process.

But how can there be true empowerment, true internal commitment, when there is no guesswork, when allowable variations are small, and operating limits tightly defined? Because tight controls reduce the need for a lot of checking, employees can feel secure and confident that they will not be unfairly dealt with, so long as they follow the dictates of the processes and respect the small variances and operating limits. But this kind of security is empowering only to individuals who have chosen to be pawns of this form of empowerment. Such people accept defined limits precisely because, if they respect them, they will be left alone and not required to question anything. In other words, they are safe from being personally responsible. Such 'going by the book' may lead to competent performance, but it neither reflects nor creates internal commitment and empowerment.

A second example consists of a gap between the values ostensibly espoused and those actually observed. An executive described as an exemplar change leader tells the story that she brought her people together to find ways to cut costs. The group is broken into smaller work groups. Hours later they return. The results, to her mind, are outstanding. Indeed, 'they knocked my socks off'. If we analyse what she said before the breakup into small groups, we find the following. First, she described the situation as serious. Second, she warned that people could lose their jobs. Third, she was sure that they could come up with solutions that were acceptable to top management. This type of participation reminds me of the description made by another change leader in a different company. He called it 'centrally controlled cooperation' (Argyris 2000).

A third example is of change leaders dealing with resistance to their programs for participation and involvement. After several workshops, the line managers concluded that Tom, the change professional in charge of the program to integrate the business and human requirements, did not know how to do the job. They also concluded that they themselves had no effective solution. They adapted by slowly withdrawing from the workshops. They created their own meetings intended to meet the new production standards. They stopped inviting Tom, who felt betrayed. He organized one final meeting. According to Tom, the session began with a considerable degree of participation. When the line managers told him that they doubted his competence and their own to achieve the goals of integration, Tom responded that the purpose of the participatory session was to solve this problem. He argued that, as long as they were sincere in wanting to solve the problems they could, through participation, come up with solutions. The line managers questioned this claim, labeling it a strategy of the blind leading the blind. Tom became increasingly upset. According to his own description, he became more unilaterally controlling and blaming the line managers for the failure. When Tom met adversity he acted in the very ways that he condemned in others (Argyris 2000). So do other change professionals. For example, I have cited the case of Tom in three different seminars with senior change professionals. I acted as Tom, asking for advice on how he could have dealt more effectively with the line managers' resistance. In all cases, the change professionals reported that I role-played Tom fairly. Yet, in all cases, as Tom said, he was not getting the help he needed. The change professionals acted toward him with the same defensive patterns that they had advised Tom not to use with the line managers (Argyris 2000).

A fourth example consists of a new factory in which the best ideas in employee participation and empowerment were to be used to design and manage the work. There was much enthusiasm on the part of management and the employees. The routine nature of jobs was reduced. Employees were given genuine opportunities to shape their lives. However, these positive results were limited, but not because the management and the workers wanted to limit them. The big barrier was that no one could make the new ideas work so that the production and quality goals could be met without introducing measuring instruments and control procedures that were indeed consistent with traditional management: the very type of management the program was intended to replace (Perry 1984).

I believe that employees are not duped by the hype. They understand that management has positive intentions. They feel sad and bewildered, however, that management is so blind to the fact that their efforts to overcome the problems are, to date, superficial. For example, their boss tells them that the success of the new ideas for solving important business problems is due to their involvement, and that that in turn rests on the opportunity given to them to participate. They are sad and bewildered because their boss does not include as a key factor in the success his own announcement that their jobs are at stake.

Workers do understand the attempts to make work more humane. They respond cooperatively. As we shall see, they also understand that there are limits to participation because the ideas for genuine integration of the business and the human sides are themselves premature and their ability to implement them limited. They view the change programs as valuable in reducing routines and providing them with opportunities to be more in control of their work lives. They are, however, frustrated with the hype around the programs and what they see as management's blindness to the impact of the hype.

I suggest that workers are quite reality-centered. The new capitalism is not, as Sennett claims, 'ineligible' to employees. It does not make them unduly anxious. So far, the experiments to make organizations more flexible and more participatory have had limited success (Argyris 2000; Beatty and Schachter 2002; Case 1999; Gibson and Tesone 2001; Grint and Case 1998; Heller 1998; Heller *et al.* 1998; Mills and Ungson 2003; Lincoln, Ackers, and Wilkinson 2002).

Sennett (1998) claims that these types of programs contribute to the corrosion of character. It is difficult to arrive at this conclusion if employees (1) are not seduced by hype, (2) are able to distinguish between the positive and negative features of the programs, and (3) are willing to speak out about their bogus qualities. Cannot one conclude that employees are reality-centered? If so, how does this illustrate the corrosion of character?

I believe that key to understanding this difference in views is that Sennett proposes a particular definition of character. 'Character is expressed by loyalty and mutual commitment or by the practice of delayed gratification for the sake of a future end' (1998: 10). Understandably, Sennett then asks how workers can maintain long-term values of commitment and loyalty in the midst of being managed by superiors dedicated to the short-term outlook characteristic of the new capitalism. Interestingly, Frese *et al.* (1996) report that work initiative is greater among West German than East German employees. West German employees exhibit more long-term self-starting behavior and personal responsibility than East German employees.

I suggest that Sennett's definition of character is problematic. First, it is possible that the employees see the inconsistency between management's espousal of long-term commitment and their theory-in-use focusing on short-term commitment. They do not take the former seriously, and pay attention to the latter. Their character is not corroded; indeed, their understanding helps to reduce the embarrassment management may feel if it became aware of what it was skillfully unaware of. From this perspective, employees are exhibiting compassion and concern.

The second problem is that the causal attribution of corrosion of character assumes that the employees can be duped or unfairly coerced. Employees are seen as hopelessly manipulated, as weak, and as pawns. This interpretation is consistent with the over-socialized view of human beings.

The third problem with the way Sennett defines character is that it permits the conclusion to be drawn, as Sennett does, that the old capitalism did not corrode character because it encouraged long-term commitment and the pursuit of long-term goals, while encouraging delayed gratification. It did so while maintaining unilateral control of Model I and organizational defensive routines. Thus, this definition bypasses the problems that dominate organizations.

Sennett's views are consistent with those of many top managers. For example, the author describes an employee, called Enrico, who lived under the old capitalism that made it possible for him to have a 'secure linear life', to predict when he would retire and how much money he would have. Permitting employees to order their lives in this manner encouraged the development of self-respect. Is not this logic consistent with management values? I can imagine an executive telling Enrico that he should be thankful for his 'secure linear life'.

There is a deeper problem with the claim that the old capitalism produced a sense of self-respect. The quality of self-respect varies with how it is generated. The respect, in this case, is generated by external commitment. Management is responsible for producing the features of the secure life. Such self-respect induces loyalty through dependence; the employees are not causally responsible for their security but they do feel secure. They are grateful for management's policies. Does this not corrode character? It may, but it is not the character defined by the author.

The fourth problem is that self-respect and commitment to others generated by processes of external commitment are limited to the setting in which it is produced. Such self-respect should not transfer to other contexts. For example, Enrico (the father) had self-respect, but he had no problem in disrespecting blacks, non-Italian foreigners, and most of all middle-class people who treated him 'as a zero'. They were responsible for actions and attitudes with which he, Enrico, did not agree. He was committed to laboring peacefully with these people as long as he could distance himself from them and cover up his feelings of being victimized by them. Enrico's commitment to them was external.

Rico, Enrico's son, did not agree with his father's bigotry. Rico was a success; he was in the midst of developing a new consulting business. But he expressed anxiety and fear about making it, and also experienced challenges that required the use of many of his abilities. He knew that he was largely responsible for the outcome. These are the conditions of internal commitment; Rico's self-respect was based on what he thought and how he acted (see Box 2.1).

Like his father, Rico was worried about spending enough time with his children. Unlike his father, he was also concerned about his wife having a genuine opportunity to follow her career. Rico's life was full of pressures that, at times, exhausted him.

In the past two decades I have observed young professionals in consulting firms. Their lives are full of pressure and worries similar to those expressed by Rico (Argyris 1993; 2000). They do experience exhaustion, but not because the work is demeaning; their exhaustion is, more often, exhilarating. Yet they remain highly committed to long-term goals and to delaying gratification in order to build a successful company of which they can be proud.

Box 2.1. External and internal commitment

External commitment	Internal commitment
Perform as required.	Perform as required and keep alert to changing the requirements.
Hold management responsible for defining the work requirements and enabling the employees to achieve them.	Seek joint responsibility for defining work requirements and enabling conditions.
Hold management responsible for identifying and correcting gaps and errors.	Hold oneself responsible for identifying and correcting gaps and errors.
Hold management responsible for defining fair financial compensation.	Seek to influence the definition of financial compensation and seek non-monetary compensation.
Depend on management. Be a pawn.	Depend on oneself. Be an originator.
Deny any personal responsibility for choosing external commitment and dependence on management.	Accept personal responsibility and seek to choose internal commitment.
Inquire into the way they reason as being unfair, if not a sign of mistrust.	Encourage inquiry into and testing of ideas.
Fear making oneself vulnerable lest one will also feel weak.	Seek making oneself vulnerable in ways that make one feel strong.

Both of these stances will permit them some day to cash in their 'sweat equity' and become wealthy. They also remain committed to their families. As the firm becomes more successful, they plan and implement more quality time with their families. No matter how busy they are and how much traveling they are doing, if serious problems arise at home they stop their work to pay full attention to solving these problems. Moreover, they know that they are supported by their fellow consultants and by formal and informal company policies.

If I understand Professor Sennett correctly, Enrico has not experienced a corrosion of character, but his son has. It would be helpful to understand why Enrico does not experience a corrosion of character, yet is described as being a bigot. Also, Enrico's future may be relatively certain and predictable; his self-respect may be sound; yet he is at the mercy of the hierarchy in his workplace. Enrico deals with this by holding management responsible for certainty and self-respect; he distances himself from being respons-ible for the 'good' features of his work life because he is, in fact, not responsible. He is externally committed.

Rico is internally committed to his work and to his family, and is loyal to both. The tensions that rise from striving to meet both commitments are great, but so are the pay-offs if he succeeds. Hence he is dedicated to long-run goals and to delaying gratifica-tion. Is his character being corroded?

Professor Sennett describes the views of some IBM executives who say that the younger employees are committed neither to long-run range goals nor to delaying gratification. The author attributes this to the fact that the company is forever reinventing and changing itself. How, he asks, can a company dedicated to a short-term time perspective expect individuals to show long-term commitment?

I have had the opportunity to work with IBM for several decades. I would agree with the IBM executives when they described many of the young employees as self-centered and having a short time perspective. But, in my experience, the young professionals devel-oped these values long before they entered the organization. They no longer valued security such as that personified by IBM and 'Ma Bell.' Indeed, IBM and other companies changed their policies in order to recruit these new professionals.

It is my hypothesis that the young people became more self-centered as work requirements changed from 'hiring a hand' to 'hiring a mind'. The more companies' successes depended upon information to succeed, the more the young people came to believe that they were in the driver's seat. They could plan their careers and change them as they wished.

These attitudes are especially strong in organizations that are founded on information technologies, especially the dotcom companies. Years ago, it was not unusual to visit such companies and to see employees wearing T-shirts that condemned bureaucracies. This bravado ended as their profit margins declined, and collapsed when many dotcom companies failed to achieve their performance and profit goals.

This is not to say that IBM and other companies do not have many employees who value the security, the certainty, and the linear life. The features of the old capitalism still exist for many employees. That is why many companies focus on such practices as job enlargement, participation, and self-management and empowerment. The espoused rationale of these programs was to develop internal commitment.

Sennett suggests that information technology programs designed to decentralize control actually centralize it in a more pervasive and insidious manner. I agree that information technology can be used in such a way to centralize control. Again, it is important to examine the theory-in-use being used. For example, the fundamental assumption of human beings using Model I is that truth is a good idea as long as it does not threaten their Model I theories-in-use and the organizational defensive routines. Information technology is based on a notion that is testable, namely, that truth is a good idea. 'Garbage in, garbage out.'

However, information technology can be used to decentralize in order to give people at the lower ranks greater control over their work activities. This can occur because sophisticated information technology makes actions and processes transparent. When performance results are transparent, top executives find it difficult to hide from their boards. Indeed, they may also fear that the lower levels could use the computerized results to challenge top management's performance. Increasingly, thoughtful executives deal with this possibility by making the results available to all levels. One chief executive officer showed me a computer printout that documented the previous day's performance in fifty-four locations throughout the world. He also told me that this information was available to all levels of the managerial hierarchy, so that they could use the information to make their own corrections, including possible corrections of actions at his office and other locations.

This capability created by information technology can be used to test Professor Sennett's hypothesis that top management's claim that they set the goals and those below can choose how to achieve them is specious, and also his claim that top management promotes goals that are beyond the immediate capabilities of the lower levels. These claims can be tested by the information provided by information technology. In this connection it is interesting to note that an analysis of the IT revolution provides examples of the positive consequences being suggested (*Economist* 2002).

To summarize, all organizations face the problem of obtaining employee commitment. The historical strategy was one of external commitment;[1] employees were rewarded for performing as required, for accepting that management was responsible for defining the work requirements, for willingly submitting to and becoming dependent upon those in control. Management strategy was to make employees 'over-socialized'.

It became increasingly clear that external commitment implemented through the use of Model I and protected by organizational defensive routines resulted in organizations lacking the flexibility and initiative required in a world of global competition. Management became increasingly aware of the value of emphasizing

---

[1] For a review of the research on internal and external commitment, see Cameron and Pierce (2001).

internal commitment, under which there would be more joint responsibility for defining work requirements, for detecting and correcting errors, for greater initiative, and for personal accountability. Management created programs that officially espoused these features. The difficulty, I suggest, is that the Model I theory-in-use dominated the design and execution of such programs, and so the degree of internal commitment allowed was limited. The result was an inconsistency between espoused theory and theory-in-use that led to only limited improvements in performance results in the short run. In the long run it led to programs that became fads.

THE CORROSION OF CHARACTER IN SOCIALIST COUNTRIES

If it is true that the fundamental causes of conflict between individuals and organizations are the division of labor, the hierarchy, the Model I theories-in-use, and organizational defensive routines, then they should be found in other countries with different espoused values. Scholars have long maintained that there was little difference between socialistic and capitalist bureaucratic structures (Gouldner 1950). Lawrence and Vlacoutsicos (1990) report that Russian factories were organized into hierarchies. According to Sköldberg (2002), Weber believed that bureaucratic organization is always technically superior to all other forms of organization. He claimed that bureaucracy functioned equally well in private capitalist companies and socialist ones. Indeed, a 'functioning socialism requires a more developed bureaucracy than capitalism' (Sköldberg 2002: 68).

Berliner (1957) and Mead (1951) also maintained that socialist and capitalist organizations faced similar problems. Mead pointed out that Soviet theories of industrial organization insisted that organization could be imposed where there was little doubt that the top is in command. Moreover, the workers were expected to respond with total devotion and spontaneity. Sköldberg concludes that bureaucracy results in a system of domination that is practically indestructible. Individual bureaucrats cannot wriggle out of the bureaucratic apparatus into which they have been harnessed. Bureaucrats are like small cogs in a ceaselessly moving mechanism that drives them to perform according to bureaucratic rules. Jobs are defined in the light of Taylorisitic molecularized generalized requirements. The rule cannot dispense with or replace the bureaucratic apparatus once it exists. Order is maintained through obedience.

There is also a new socialism whose organizations are striving to become increasingly competitive within Russia and globally. As in the case of the new capitalism, they emphasize flexibility, initiative, and empowerment. Their theory of leadership is consistent with Model I. Not surprisingly, many of their programs to enhance these new features are also manipulative. For example, Puffer, McCarthy, and Nwumov (2000) report that many programs are now available to help managers realize that hitherto they were acculturated to be passive and not energized to learn. Many managers attend these programs where they are told that such attitudes are wrong and must be corrected.

Leetis (1985), reviewing the Soviet literature on management style, provided us with some insights into the kind of messages that may be communicated. For example, the fundamental task of Soviet management was to create a system of control in which the non-implementation of adopted decisions is impossible. The possibility that low levels of control might lead to high levels of performance was rejected. Unilateral control was necessary to overcome the fear that the employees would not react as required.

Hollingshead and Mickavilovs (2001) describe programs intended to create genuine cohesion through participation. These programs 'gave' workers pride and status; workers were called 'partners' rather than employees; team spirit was created by outings. Programs were designed to instill in people 'the impression' that this was their company, that they were part of a family.

It is one of the great ironies that socialism, which is intended to liberate workers, continues with structures and policies that are more controlling of workers than may be the case in the new capitalism (Puffer, McCarthy, and Nwumov 2000). Buraway (2001), who documents these findings, recommends that scholars who are partial to socialism, like himself, conduct research to show how socialism can improve the workers' life-work conditions. I suggest that such changes will not be liberating unless the Model I theories-in-use and organizational defensive routine (that Buraway documents) are reduced and Model II theories-in-use are strengthened.

3

Inhibiting Double-Loop Learning in Business Organizations

THE INTEL STORY

Robert Burgelman (2002*a*; 2002*b*) has written a rich description of how strategy is shaped in organizations. Although the case study concerns Intel, Burgelman claims, and I would agree, that much of the story is relevant to other organizations.

The purpose of this chapter is to suggest that Burgelman's description is incomplete if his intention is to help practitioners implement strategy effectively. As written, his advice is about structural features that enable strategy implementation. This advice, although very relevant, is abstract and not adequately related to what goes on within Intel as he describes it. I hope to show that, if he had included in his focus the theories-in-use that dominated strategy implementation at Intel, this would not only have provided to a richer description but would also have provided insights into how improvements could be made. These insights, in turn, would require alterations in the structural changes that he recommends.

The study is incomplete also from a scientific point of view. I hope to show that it does not include an explanation of the causal processes that he identifies as central. Nor are the causal processes crafted in such a way that they could be tested without reliance upon self-referential, self-sealing logic.

I begin with Burgelman's (1994) article on strategy-making at Intel roughly between 1971 and 1991. This part of the story focuses upon Intel's responses to the changing environment of its dynamic random access memory (DRAM) business and how Intel eventually exited from that business.[1]

Burgelman tells a story of mixed success and failure in organizational learning, and stresses the 'inertial' lag of formal corporate strategy in relation to shifting conditions in the competitive environment. Burgelman (1994: 24) sets out to provide 'Insight into how the internal selection environment mediates the co-evolution of industry-level sources of competitive advantage and firm-level sources of distinctive competence and into the link between corporate strategy and strategic action'. Burgelman tells the story of a twenty-year transformation in Intel's strategic practice, tracking its passage through three stages:

1. an equilibrium state, with harmony between dominant beliefs and strategic context, in which Intel thought of itself as a 'memory company' (and, more specifically, a DRAM company);
2. a transitional period of disharmony in which the basis for competitive advantage in the memory business changed, while Intel's formal strategy remained inert and momentum developed internally toward the opening up of new business opportunities; and
3. a later harmonious state in which Intel came to think of itself as a microprocessor company.

Ultimately, as Burgelman reveals, Intel learned. It learned to recognize that, through its incremental responses to challenges, mainly from Japanese competitors, it had dealt itself out of the DRAM business and should not try by massive capital investment to re-establish its position in that business. It learned to exploit the technological opportunities that came about as byproducts of its

---

[1] I draw heavily on Argyris and Schön (1996: 1–17).

experience in the DRAM business (the EPROMS development pioneered by Dov Frohman, which came about through exploration of reliability problems with Intel's MOS technology; and the new chip architecture, which grew out of a customer's request for a new chip set). These opportunities, initially recognized or tolerated by top management, were, according to Burgelman, internal variations. They were eventually selected by Intel's internal environment, and they eventually contributed to the technological basis for its microprocessor business. Intel also learned to shift its scarce manufacturing capacity from DRAM to microprocessor technology, and Intel's top management eventually learned to redefine Intel as a microprocessor company.

But, as Burgelman tells it, the Intel story is also one of failure to learn of inertial delays in learning. Burgelman (1994: 29–30) frames this side of the story in terms of six puzzling questions around which he structures his analysis. I focus on four of these:

1. Why did Intel, the first successful mover in DRAMs, fail to capitalize on and defend its early lead?
2. How did it happen that the bulk of Intel's business had shifted away from DRAMs, and DRAM market share allowed to dwindle, while top management, even in 1984, was still thinking of DRAMs as a strategic business for the company?
3. How was it possible that middle-level managers could take actions that were not in line with the official corporate strategy?
4. Why did it take Intel's top management almost a year to complete the exit from DRAMs after the November 1984 decision not to market one Meg DRAMs?

These questions point to a series of strategic mistakes that Intel seemingly made and to inertial delays in its attempts to reconcile its formal strategy to changing competitive conditions and to convert its new strategic intent into action. Such mistakes and delays are to be understood as failures in the timely detection and correction of significant errors (surprises or mismatch of outcomes to expectations). However, there is some ambiguity in Burgelman's treatment of his puzzles. He certainly does frame them in terms of Intel's apparent failure to take effective, timely action or to match its thoughts to a changing reality. But he also suggests that in certain respects Intel's delayed responses were functional. He speculates, for example, that Intel 'would probably have done worse if it had simply divested the DRAM business and entered the new business through acquisition... [because it would have thereby] failed to capitalize on the full potential of its distinctive competencies in DRAMs, [some of which] could be effectively deployed in the microprocessor business' (1994: 52).

This ambiguity plays an important role in the discussion that follows. Burgelman's approach to his puzzles has both an historical and a systems dimension. He argues that Intel secured a strong competitive advantage in the early days of the DRAM business on the basis of its distinctive technical competence in designing, building, and manufacturing the DRAM technology. He argues further that the early successes of DRAM caused Intel's corporate strategy to be dominated by its DRAM technology. He postulates a micro-theory of success and failure along the lines of Levitt and March's (1988) competence trap: when a pattern of factors is clearly related to a firm's understanding of its success, this pattern tends to be reinforced and thus to persist even after it ceases to be effective in the competitive business environment.

Burgelman (1994: 41) describes several phenomena that reinforced established patterns associated with Intel's earlier success:

- the self-interest of business unit heads who had considerable latitude for decision-making yet had no interest in putting themselves out of business;
- the 'bounded rationality' that kept top or middle managers from anticipating the competitive market dynamics of product and manufacturing technology that would squeeze out Intel's share of the DRAM market; and
- top management's 'emotional attachment' to the DRAM business, which made it reluctant to get out of that business,

just as Ford would be reluctant to 'decide that it should get out of the car business'.

In contrast to the factors that kept Intel's top management from letting go of its attachment to the DRAM business and its image of Intel as a 'memory company', Burgelman postulates an 'internal selective environment' made up of 'structural and strategic contexts shaping strategic actions' on the part of middle managers. In the Intel case, middle managers used their discretionary freedoms to take actions that had the effect of opening up new business opportunities. For example, they pursued the development of technological offshoots of the DRAM business that would lay the groundwork for microprocessors. And they allocated scarce manufacturing capacity to favor microprocessors over DRAMs, making use of the established corporate rule that manufacturing capacity should be allocated so as to 'maximize margin-per-wafer-stare' (1994: 43), even while top management continued to support the view that Intel should remain in the DRAM business. In these and related ways, middle managers gradually undermined the position of the existing DRAM business and helped 'dissolve', as Burgelman puts it, the earlier strategic context of the firm.

Burgelman calls his perspective 'inside-out'. He tells how Intel's external business environment created conditions—changes in the market and DRAMs becoming a commodity—to which Intel responded with decreasing effectiveness. But he treats the 'inside' as crucial. Unlike other writers, especially economists, who relegate inside activities largely to a black box, Burgelman opens the box. He sees that, as Intel sought to maintain its competitive advantage by acting in ways that were consistent with its perception of its distinctive competence, it did and failed to do things that actually led to its competitive disadvantage. For example, although Intel's top managers did realize dial DRAM had gone from a premium-priced to a commodity product (the price signals were rather clear), they persisted in believing that they could regain the lead by applying their traditional strengths in process technology to come up with innovative products that would be premium-priced niche products at first but would have to be adopted eventually by the entire market. The moment DRAMs became a commodity, Intel's strategy of being the first to introduce premium-priced products into the market became outmoded. Yet top management acted as if this were not the case.

In addition, Burgelman suggests that middle managers believed top management was closed to constructive confrontation about its emotional attachment to the DRAM business. From our perspective, the middle managers were making attributions about top management's openness to learning. From the data in the case, we infer that they never tested these attributions. In discussion, Burgelman confirmed this inference. He said, in effect,

Given the status and power of the process development people, anyone who went into a meeting to propose a view different from theirs would be unlikely to carry the day. Furthermore, top managers were seen by middle managers as believing that Intel could not make changes away from DRAMs. Top management was seen as unsure.

This behavior provides a partial explanation of top management's 'blindness': they were never confronted with data that would help them realize the impact of their behavior. Burgelman's explanation focuses on the top management's uncertainty and, in the face of that uncertainty, its resistance to change. We would focus, in addition, on middle managers' actions that helped to keep top management from realizing the full implications of the shift in the DRAM business, which, in turn, let top managers act in ways middle managers explained as resistance to change. Burgelman focuses on the self-sealing processes of the top managers, not on those created by the middle managers. If an intervention were designed to interrupt the limited learning processes revealed by the Intel case, it would fail if it were one-sided.

Burgelman reports that Intel's top management encouraged constructive confrontation. Andy Grove (then chief operating officer, COO, now CEO) told managers at all levels that decisions should be data-driven and that power and emotional biases should play no role in decision-making. We hypothesize, nevertheless, that middle managers' attributions to top management were not openly discussed and analyzed in ways that would test their validity and allow them to be corrected if they proved mistaken.

Burgelman (1994) describes an additional domain of undiscussables. He notes that, when DRAMs became a commodity, manufacturing capability became the dominant success factor. Yet process development (TD) people continued to downgrade manufacturing and distance themselves from it. They continued to frame problems in mainly scientific terms, treating manufacturing people as 'tweakers'. The manufacturing people reacted by developing a 'not invented here' (NIH) syndrome. Gordon Moore, then CEO, reacted to this interdepartmental rivalry by placing both groups in geographical proximity in order to foster greater cooperation between them. Moore had experienced similar problems at Fairchild and wanted to avoid them now at Intel: an attempt to learn from his earlier experience. Burgelman reports that this strategy was at first effective but became much less effective when competitive pressures made the differences between TD and manufacturing much more salient.

Burgelman also observes organizational defenses at work in the relationship between upper-level middle managers and the Board. By 1980, when the company's total market share in DRAMs was less than 3 per cent, these managers saw the writing on the wall. Yet they would learn of board meetings where Moore, then CEO, and Gelbach, the head of marketing, would defend continued expenditures on DRAM: Moore, because he saw DRAMs as the company's 'technology driver', and Gelbach, because he believed Intel had to offer its customers a one-stop semiconductor shopping list. Andy Grove (then COO) remained silent. As a result of such board-level interactions, middle managers were frustrated.

These multi-leveled undiscussables reinforced by organizational defensive routines would make Grove's advocacy of constructive confrontation sound more like espoused theory than theory-in-use, namely, his view that one of the toughest challenges is to make people see that their self-evident truths are no longer true, or organizations should practice creative destruction of routines that are no longer effective.

Burgelman told me that top management recognized the organizational defensiveness, which they saw as existing primarily among some middle managers. As far as we can tell, top management did not examine this defensiveness directly and forthrightly with the middle managers. If so, we have top managers acting to reinforce middle managers' unawareness of their impact on those at the top.

Top management attempted to deal with interdepartmental conflicts by bringing departments into geographical proximity, defining rules to reduce the conflicts, and providing incentive systems that would do so. Over the long haul, none of these strategies worked, although some of them were effective in the first instance.

Burgelman's Analysis Analyzed

There is only partial truth in Burgelman's hypothesis that top management persisted in its commitment to the DRAM business because of emotional attachment to it and uncertainty about its importance. What is needed is an explanation of how subordinates colluded with their superiors to create domains of undiscussables that would inhibit learning around these issues.

I agree with Burgelman that we should also try to understand how it comes about that organizations do not detect and correct significant errors, but we seek to go further and want to understand how it comes about that Intel or other organizations are unaware that they are unable to detect and correct significant errors. The inability to detect and correct error is skilled because we can connect it to a theory-in-use; hence, it is skilled incompetence. The existence of skilled incompetence means unawareness of the inability, and unawareness is also connected to a theory-in-use—hence, it is skilled unawareness.

What is included in this concept of 'emotional attachment'? What is the theory-in-use that produces such behavior? Is Burgelman using the concept to mean that emotional attachment always causes blindness? If not, what would be the difference between the two types of emotional attachment? How could the conditions named in his four puzzles hold when top management espoused a theory of management intended to prevent them from occurring?

Solving this puzzle would require much more directly observable data about what was actually said when people at Intel discussed these issues. For example, how did the middle-level managers craft their conversations? Did they ease in so much that their points were obscured? Or did they become so confrontational that the others could discount their views because they were obviously emotional?

Did the middle managers engage top managers in a dialogue about the attributions they were making about them? Did they explore their claims that these issues were undiscussable, and their undiscussability also undiscussable? Did they explore their claims that, even if these issues were discussed, top management would be uninfluenced? Did they ever inquire whether the top managers were unaware of the 'blindness' that middle managers attributed to them?

Burgelman (1994) states that Grove did not at first believe that the lag time was as long or the inertia as deep as Burgelman concludes they were. To his credit, however, Grove conducted his own investigation and found that Burgelman's estimate was better than his own. Grove also questioned the relevant players and, months after the decision to exit the DRAM business, they gave him information they had not told him or that he had not listened to before.

Burgelman's explanations of the puzzling phenomena of delayed or failed organizational learning do not account for such phenomena developing in an organization in which cultural context, top management support, and the sheer brightness of the Intel managers would seem to militate against their occurring.

If Intel failed to capitalize on and defend its early lead in the DRAM business, for example, what actually produced the failure? To say that it was top management's emotional attachment to DRAMs is to pinpoint a small group within an abstract explanation. How did management actually behave? How did middle-level management confront top management's emotional attachment, if it actually did? How did it attempt to change it? In other words, it is possible that the puzzling phenomena of delay and inertia were caused both by top management's emotionalism and blindness and by middle managers' ways of dealing with them, that is, by bypassing these issues and acting as if they were not doing so.

An operational definition of a more complete explanation of the puzzles could be used to design action to change the causes of inertia. The causes Burgelman identifies, such as top management's emotional attachment to DRAMs, interdepartmental rivalries between TD and manufacturing, and self-reinforcing processes that maintained outmoded strategic frames, are stated at a level of abstraction that cannot be used to change the organization to enable it to learn to detect and correct its errors.

Burgelman concludes his analysis by advancing a set of propositions, some of which, in the light of this analysis, are somewhat incomplete. His first proposition states:

The stronger a firm's distinctive technological competence, the stronger the firm's tendency to continue to rely on it in the face of industry-level changes in the basis of competitive advantage. (1994: 48)

This proposition holds or holds more strongly whenever organizational defensive routines at top- or middle-management levels or between departments reinforce the failure to face up to industry-level changes and to legitimize the bypassing and cover-up of such reinforcement.

Burgelman's third proposition states:

Firms whose internal selection criteria accurately reflect external selection pressures are more likely to strategically exit from some businesses than firms whose internal selection criteria do not accurately reflect external selection pressures. (1994: 50)

We would add:

Firms whose internal selection criteria reflect and deal with external selection pressure should be observed to have minimal defensive routines (of the sort we have described earlier).

Burgelman's sixth proposition states:

Firms that have strategically exited from a business are likely to have a better understanding of the links between their distinctive competences and the basis of competition in the industries in which they remain active than firms that have not strategically exited from a business. (1994: 50)

This proposition is valid under the condition that organizational defensive routines dominate the examination of errors that are embarrassing and threatening to key players. It should not hold for firms that are not dominated by such defensive routines; these firms should have a better understanding before, rather than after, exit.

In sum, Burgelman's analysis of the Intel case focuses on puzzles rooted mainly in the organization's failures to detect and correct error:

- its failure to follow up its early lead in the DRAM business;
- its delay in matching its strategic ideas and self-image to the changing business reality; and
- its inertia in completing its exit from the DRAM business once it had decided to do so.

Burgelman's explanations of these puzzles hinge on the phenomena of top management's emotional attachment to the DRAM business, its bounded rationality and blindness concerning the mismatch of its strategic context to the changing business reality, the power and self-interest of business-unit managers associated with the DRAM business, and the rivalry between technological development and manufacturing departments. But each of these causes raises questions related to another puzzle: how did it happen that Intel's managers were unaware of their inability to detect and correct their errors? This question points, in turn, to the layer of organizational phenomena that we regard as critically important both to the explanation of existing patterns of organizational learning and to the design of interventions aimed at changing those patterns, that is, the organizational defensive routines that constrained interpersonal inquiry between top- and middle-level managers, and between departments, thereby reinforcing a lack of awareness of the gap between Intel's strategic context and its changing business reality.

In a private communication to the author, Burgelman stresses the uncertainty with which Intel's top managers were dealing at the time they were grappling with the possibility of exiting from the DRAM business. He argues that their inertial delays and the defensive routines that reinforced those delays were actually functional since they enabled Intel to exploit in its microprocessors certain technological advances made by the DRAM process developers and also to prevent TD/DRAM people from leaving the company. He observes:

I like to emphasize that one of the key points of my study is that it is very difficult for top and middle managers to examine at length what the strategic situation is [that is] faced by an organization in very dynamic environments. So much is going on simultaneously that the kind of exhaustive 'airing out' of the strategic situation is probably unachievable. So, while I believe your hypothesis is a plausible one and that perhaps more effort should be spent on airing out strategic situations, I also believe (1) that we do not know enough yet about how 'defensive routines' come about (perhaps my study contributes to precisely that!) and (2) that it is improbable that there is no cost at all associated with removing defensive routines. I submit that trying to remove defensive routines altogether might very well paralyze organizations operating in dynamic environments.

In this passage, Burgelman argues, as he does later on as well, that in dynamic and uncertain environments there may be considerable value in 'strategic neglect'.

The weakness in this argument is as follows. Inertial delays in a firm's response to a mismatch between its formal strategy and its actual strategic situation may be retrospectively discovered, on occasion, to be functional. But these delays may just as easily prove to be dysfunctional. How are managers to distinguish between functional and dysfunctional strategic neglect so long as they keep themselves unaware of their discordant beliefs and keep the crucial and threatening issues undiscussable?

Why, moreover, should we assume that the opening up of defensive routines would make it impossible to realize deliberately the same benefits as those that were inadvertently realized (through lack of awareness)? For example, Intel's top management could have chosen to keep its TUDRAM capability on the very grounds of its uncertainty about its possible future utility, even in the face of a clear decision to exit the DRAM business.

Why then should the airing out of the strategic situation have to be exhaustive (certainly a recipe for paralysis!) when it could be limited to just those dilemmas that constituted the main bone of contention between top- and upper-level middle managers? One need not know just how defensive routines come about (although we believe our theory offers some insight into that question) in order to see how they constrain productive inquiry into critically important strategic issues. The questions that are raised above are generated by viewing the Intel story from a Theory of Action perspective. The claim is that the dominant leadership theory-in-use by top management and by their reports is Model I. Model I leadership actions, in turn, produce organizational defensiveness. The organizational defensive routines feed back to reinforce Model I theories-in-use. This creates a circular causal process that produces self-fulfilling, self-sealing processes. These processes, in turn, produce an ultra-stable state that is anti-double-loop learning.

Intel's management acknowledges the existence of these defensive routines. Its explanation is that defensive routines are predictable because of human nature reinforced by the omnipresence of organizational behavior systems that reinforce these routines. Such an explanation produces and reinforces two consequences. First, the logic behind the causal explanation is consistent with Model I defensive reasoning and is therefore self-referential. The test for validity that can be developed by using the logic is not truly independent of the reasoning behind the claims. Hence it produces self-sealing processes.

The second consequence is that, if one believes that the above defensiveness is an integral unchangeable feature of individuals, groups, inter-groups, and organizations, then the solution is to invent structural policies and practices that prevent these defensive routines from developing or from becoming too powerful. The description by Burgelman illustrates that these defensive routines have not been reduced significantly by the structural solutions. The second story by Burgelman, to which I will turn, illustrates that these organizational defensive routines at Intel remain powerful or may have even increased in power over two decades. All this occurred while management was introducing, revising, and strengthening the structural solutions.

This does not mean that the structural solutions are not helpful. It means that the solutions are probably more limited than the man agement believes. Moreover, the hypothesis upon which these solutions are derived—that you can't change these defensive actions—is implemented in such ways that it is not testable.

The problem, therefore, is that these structural solutions provide a false sense of security about solving the problems that produce counterproductive consequences to their own management policies and practices.

The argument so far is that Intel's capacity for double-loop learning is non-trivially hindered by the ways that its leaders manage and by the policies and practices that they define. The leaders espouse Model II leadership strategies. Their theory-in-use is Model I, but they appear unaware of the discrepancy. One reason is that their subordinates collude to keep them blind. Another reason is that they put organizational policies and practices in place that make it difficult to create the conditions that they espouse (for example, financial allocations and controls).

Burgelman (2002a) has recently written a book that provides much more detailed and systematic descriptions of the structural and interpersonal activities that went on in Intel during their strategy-making. Although the book does not contain the relatively directly observable data that is ideally required to make inferences about theories-in-use, it does contain descriptions from interviews about actions as observed by others. From these descriptions it is possible to infer patterns that provide a more credible basis for the theories-in-use at management levels. Burgelman also includes examples of the consequences of these Model I theories-in-use on the development of new products and companies as well as the trust, openness, and competence for double-loop learning.

Grove's Leadership Actions

I focus on Grove because, according to Burgelman, he was the key leader at Intel during the several decades upon which the book focuses. There are fewer illustrations where the other top executives differ in the degree to which they adhere to Model I. I could not find one illustration of leading human beings that was based on Model II.

Before I illustrate these claims, I should like to point out that there were actions consistent with productive reasoning. These actions occurred when the learning required to solve the problems was primarily technical. Whenever the dialogue was about microprocessors, for example, it was informed by rigorous inquiry, which in turn was based upon scientific knowledge relevant to microprocessing. The participants, for example, were required to, and did, make premises explicit; and they made their inferences and conclusions explicit. They also crafted them in such a way that they could be tested using logic other than the one used by the producer of the conclusion. This emphasis on productive reasoning is a central feature of Model II theory-in-use.

Competence in productive reasoning was not, as far as I could determine, used when it came to leading and learning about human issues such as trust, openness, honesty, and courage. The reasoning about these issues was largely defensive. For example, the premises used by Grove about effective leadership were subjective and tacit. His conclusions were crafted in such ways that they were testable only by using the logic that he used to create them in the first place. This is self-referential logic, which Grove would not, I believe, tolerate in the technical/scientific domain. Moreover, organizational policies and rules were created that supported Model I defensive reasoning in the leadership/learning domain, and organizational structural features were created to prevent genuine double-loop learning and to strengthen the systematic blindness. In fairness, it is important to keep in mind that the ultra-stable state against double-loop learning is not unique to Intel and its executives, but is characteristic of the great majority of organizations.

Intel was more unusual in the technical/scientific domain, where the rules about implementation and rigorous reasoning were much clearer and more explicit, and were required by top management. The Intel executives were highly skillful at single-loop learning. The detailed description, for example, of moving away from DRAM (integrated circuits) toward microprocessors illustrates that the movement was based on hundreds of incidents and experiments. The management was vigilant about learning from its actions. It sought to identify errors and to correct them in such ways that the solutions persisted.

The governing values of Intel included (1) being the best in whatever goal it chose to achieve, (2) focusing on products that promised large returns, and (3) providing products with superior quality and safety. These governing values were in turn supported by quantitative financial policies and practices intended to monitor top management's performance.

To put this another way, there are two kinds of error. The first is error due to ignorance. Such errors are detected and corrected by vigilant striving to reduce ignorance while producing valid solutions that are implementable. This requires, as the Intel experience illustrates, continual focus on learning. This in turn requires that the individuals be skilled at learning and up to date on the technical/scientific knowledge that is relevant to microprocessors. Intel executives had or were educated in the competences required to perform these types of learning. Moreover, they were rewarded for using the competences wisely. All this occurred in the service of the already defined governing values. This means that, although the learning was massive, it was single-loop learning. No double-loop learning was required because the governing values were clearly defined, the competences were there, and the governing values were not questioned.

When it comes to building trust, honesty, courage, inter-group collaboration, and acting in accordance with what they believe is correct rather than what they are ordered to do (all espoused by Intel), the errors that occurred were not due to ignorance, but were of the second kind: produced by design. All the actions that have been and will be described that enhance defensive reasoning and actions are due to following Model I. Designed actions that violate the formal managerial values of the organization required that they be covered up. Cover-up, in turn, required that it be covered up itself.

Moreover, the meaning of the governing values differs significantly different according to whether one uses Model I or Model II. For example, the requirements that Intel espouses are consistent with Model II. The actual behavior that can be observed in implementing these virtues is consistent with Model I. Senior executives are unaware of the discrepancies that they produce. Moreover, their unawareness is supported by managerial practices that suppress the evidence of the unawareness. For example, structural solutions are adequate to achieve actions that are consistent with Model II when the problems are technical. I should like to illustrate this diagnosis by examining the espoused theory and the theory-in-use of the leadership actions of Grove as described by Burgelman (2002b).

My understanding of what Grove espoused about effective leadership in organizations includes the following:

1. Hire very bright people who know the technology and science relevant to their tasks. Moreover, they should be dedicated to and competent in being at the intellectual forefront of their technical/scientific domain.
2. Hire individuals who have a lot of energy to work very hard and who are dedicated to the governing values of Intel.
3. Manage individuals' performance by focusing on the details of their performance.
4. Reward individuals' performances by using strict quantitative procedures that are credible and transparent.
5. Manage the actions of individuals by focusing on content and not style.

6. Allocate scarce organizational resources by using strict quantitative models that are credible and transparent.
7. Hire executives who have the courage of their convictions. The rule is: do what is right, not what you are ordered to do.
8. Hire executives capable of crafting positions that are rigorously sound and implementable. Executives should be good at making clear distinctions and not soft-money claims.

Jackson (1997) states that Grove used constructive criticism and tight, detailed control in managing Intel. The rules of constructive criticism were that Intel people get problems out into the open so that they could be discussed and solved without arousing personal animosities. In practice 'constructive confrontation' dialogue was 'abrupt, aggressive and interrogatory' (Jackson 1997: 110).

Grove controlled his managers by the use of detailed budgets, which, if changed, required rigorous explanations and defense.

In Grove's leadership and theory-in-use, the following prescriptions stand out:

1. Advocate your position, make evaluations or attributions in ways that are clear, explicit, and in the service of winning the argument. Sell and persuade. For example, be very detail-driven, see issues as black and white, and expect clear-cut choices. Nothing mushy, like 'it seems that' or 'perhaps'. If individuals get into an argument, listen in order to get their inconsistencies and gaps, point them out, and expect them to resolve them or 'I will'. Or synthesize the views in a coherent whole that is consistent with those views.
2. Advocate courage, honesty, and trust in ways that inhibit these features. If this self-defeating behavior is exposed, blame it on the actions of others. For example, deal with lack of courage and mistrust by espousing the opposite and do so in ways that make it difficult for others to expose the inconsistency. If inconsistency is exposed, explain it by 'I am forced to do this by others' actions'.
3. Use rules of effective leadership that keep you in unilateral control. For example, do not trust people to keep their promises; therefore, monitor their actions frequently. Claim

that the follow-up is not in the service of unilateral control as much as it is holding others responsible for their promises. Solidify and 'vectorize'. 'Vectorize' means establishing a direction, a point of application that is filled with powerful energy and commitment. Grove emphasized that Job 1 (microprocessors) was *the* focus. Strive to educate those who appear to disagree. If education does not work, then remove those who are not cooperative or who will delay progress.

4. Be demanding but fair. 'Demanding' means very high standards and very hard work. 'Fair' means testing what he advocates and what he criticizes as long as the issues are about substance. Exclude discussion of leadership style and seek organizational mechanisms with which to bypass style problems (Burgelman 2002).

5. Send mixed messages about effective leadership, act as if they are not mixed, make these features undisscussable, and make the undiscussability undiscussable.

The first safeguards are governing values. The theory-in-use governing variables for these action strategies were as follows:

- Protect and expand Intel's core microprocessing business. Be at the forefront of the science and technology that is involved. Maintain architectural leadership.
- Be a world-class manufacturing organization.
- Emphasize product quality and large margins.

These governing values provided constraints within which chaos could exist and also guidelines when it was time to rein in the chaos. They provided the rationale for giving individuals the space to take initiatives. They also provided the guidelines for the kind of people to hire, the rules and measurements for evaluating performances, the allocation of scarce resources, and the kinds of education they may require.

When it came to consider entering a new type of business, a 'new' company was created. It was free to take the actions deemed necessary, within three constraints.

1. It had to use the current human resources and finance rules and regulations.
2. It was not allowed to hire existing Intel people for one year.
3. It had to adhere to pay-as-you-go financial policies that were much more strict and limiting than were used by the existing company. One important reason for these limits was that the criteria for success in Intel were: to generate a multi-billion-dollar business, to have a proven model, to generate a sustainable and large market share. Although the new company was not expected to fulfill these criteria overnight, the senior execu- tives monitored progress. They watched to see how well the new leaders vectorized their organization.

The head of the 'new' company, Frank Gill, eventually faced several important challenges. First, the financial constraints placed on the company were seen by him and his top executives as unfair, since they would limit the scope and speed of their progress. Burgelman (2002a) describes many meetings between Gill and Grove, in which Gill sought to change some of the business and financial aspects. The result was increasing defensiveness and mistrust on both sides.

For example, Grove reports that he concluded that Gill was pet-rified of him (Grove). He saw Gill as being intimidated by Grove's actions. Grove could not understand why this was the case, since he thought highly of Gill. In his opinion he was the second-best sales manager in Intel's history. He was tough; indeed, he was called 'Sluggo'.

Gill said that the historical vectorization upon Job 1 made it dif-ficult for Grove and others to discuss new business rationally and fairly. Also, he thought the planning process that Grove and other senior officials designed was not right for a new business.

Gill and other senior executives developed theory-in-use rules to deal with Grove. For example:

- Sense Grove's mood.
- Remember: if he is confused he gets tough. He bulldozes through everything in his way. He tells anyone who is in his way to get lost—to get out of the way.

- Remember, once he has made up his mind, it is difficult to change it. If he does change his mind, he often does it without acknowledging it.
- Remember Grove is unaware of his actions. Or, if he becomes aware, he will likely blame others for causing his actions.
- Keep these rules in mind when you craft your conversations with him. Do so by acting as if you are not using the rules.

Gill eventually concluded that his relationship with Grove had deteriorated beyond repair. On the surface it was cordial; but they no longer openly brainstormed or communicated freely. Gill concluded that Grove was beyond influence; he also admitted that he didn't reach out. But he gave up on trying to persuade him. He concluded that the key to success was to get results rather than discussing and resolving these issues.

Looking back, Gill reported that he wished that he had tried to control his emotions, especially his anger, because a few simple words from Grove would have resolved most of his cross-group issues. Also, he wished that he had focused harder on persuading Intel to set up another company completely separate from the existing one.

We see that Grove alleges that Gill was petrified and intimidated. But he does not test this claim. He depends for its validity upon his view of Gill, namely, that he was tough and that Grove was his best champion. This is self-referential logic and hence undermines a valid test of his attributions about Gill.

Gill claims that Grove was beyond influence and unaware that this was the case. But Gill does not test these claims. Indeed, he develops a set of skills on how to craft his dialogue with Grove that reinforces the validity of these strategies. This too is self-referential logic and hence undermines any valid test. The defensiveness between the two escalates until Grove tells Gill that he does not trust him; Gill's response is to say the same thing about Grove. Eventually Gill concludes that, given the organizational, financial, and other policy constraints, and given his irreversible conclusion about a loss of trust, he should leave. This is consistent with his view that Grove wants him to get out of the way, but, again, this is not tested with Grove.

Indeed, given each actor's Model I strategies, one could predict that, if either tried to engage these issues forthrightly, the problem would likely escalate. We have a Model I consequence of self-fulfilling prophecies and self-sealing processes. Grove's rule to focus on substance and not style creates at least two problems. The substantive issues were not, in Gill's mind, so easily separable; he could not act as competently in the substantive area as he believed he could without resolving the issues of style—the very issues that Grove rules as out of bounds.

I should like to close with Burgelman's letter, cited above. He states that he doubts that these busy executives would have the time and energy to focus success-fully on reducing their own and the company's defensive routines. Therefore, he focused on structural solutions. I believe that Grove and many of the other senior executives would agree. In my experience, this exposes the fact that the time used to defend, bypass, circumvent, and hide counterproductive activities can also be massive and costly.

Moreover, lower-level managers often express bewilderment about being told that these political games are necessary and valuable. Grove was not unaware that these counterproductive consequences existed; indeed, he believed that one of his responsibilities was to counter them by continually preaching the importance of honesty and courage: do not let the past guide the future; do not do something tomorrow just because you did it today.

His subordinates listened respectfully. They reacted privately by reinforcing their view that Grove was unaware that his preaching strategy was not working. They understood that Grove wanted them to show courage and to 'tell it like it is'. As one executive in another company once said, 'I have guts, I just don't want them spilled all over the place'.

If there exists the self-reinforcing state against double-loop learning, and if the lack of double-loop learning has the counterproductive consequences described above, then it is can be safely predicted that the massive organizational self-sealing defensive routines described by Burgelman (2002*a*: 297–301) will continue. Indeed, they have continued during the decades the book describes.

THE TAP STORY

The Intel story illustrated how defensive routines of leaders, middle management, and top management affected the implementation of the key technical scientific factors, especially their time requirements. The TAP story illustrates similar consequences but goes one step further. The authors present rich behavioral descriptions of defensive routines and how they helped to cause the failure of an important medical product.

In a noteworthy study of technological innovation in the medical field, Van de Ven and Polley (1992) set out to test the familiar adaptive model of trial-and-error learning. In its simplest form, this model holds that we persist in a course of action if we perceive its results as positive and deviate from that course if we perceive its results as negative. The authors propose to apply this model, which had previously been explored in 'unrealistic laboratory or simulation studies', to the 'highly uncertain organizational field setting' of entrepreneurs in an innovation unit (1992: 113). In certain respects, they attempt to test the model rigorously; but in other respects, at least as important, we find their treatment of organizational innovation and learning to be limited and lacking in rigor.

The authors tell two complementary stories of technological innovation. The first, articulated at a relatively high level of aggregation and couched in the language of statistical analysis, tests hypotheses derived from the adaptive learning model against the behavior of two organizational units, the 'innovation's internal management team' and the 'external resource controllers'. The second story, presented in a running narrative (but not illustrated by actual dialogue), tells how individuals behaved at key points in the innovation's trajectory. But while the authors suggest some possible causes of the behavior that resulted in limited organizational learning, they offer no coherent theory to account for it, nor do their concluding prescriptions offer much of a basis for improving it. Their article demonstrates the limits of both a high-level analysis of organizational learning and a reliance on quantitative, statistical methodology. One has the impression that, although the authors intuit the importance of their behavioral story, they have no way of explaining or getting underneath it.

Testing the Adaptive Learning Model

The subject of Van de Ven and Polley's longitudinal study is a joint venture by three corporations to create a business by developing a new medical technology called therapeutic apheresis which treats disease by removal of pathogenic blood components (1992: 98).

Aphaeresis had been around for some time, but it had not gained widespread usage because of its limited ability to remove specific components of blood. The Therapeutic Apheresis Program (TAP) centered on a device consisting of filters, pumps, and computer controls that was designed to make more specific separations possible. The joint venture partners sought to combine their respective competencies in separation techniques, pump technology, and marketing. They planned a three-phase development process:

(1) a product to compete with existing apheresis technology;
(2) an advanced product to treat specific diseases using advanced filtration modules; and
(3) the development of future apheresis technologies.

Van de Ven and Polley (1992: 99) conducted a 'real-time field study of TAP's development from October 1983 to July 1988'. They divided the innovation's eight-year trajectory into three stages:

(1) an initial three-year gestation period, culminating in a formal decision to initiate and fund the TAP innovation as a joint inter-organizational venture;

(2) a three-year expansion period aimed at producing a commercial TAP device, expanding the development program, and meeting FDA requirements; and

(3) a two-year contraction period when the TAP device entered the market, experienced product difficulties, and was terminated.

As the authors test their model of adaptive learning against the data of the TAP story, their findings vary with the three phases of development. In the gestation period, they find actions and outcomes unrelated; in the expansion period, they find them negatively related; and in the contraction period, positively related.

In the expansion period, the authors find 'little or no learning by trial and error'. Rather, negative outcomes 'led directly to continuing with the prior course of actions' which had 'no effects on subsequent assessments of positive or negative outcomes nor on changes in goals or criteria' (1992: 104). The authors interpret this 'direct negative relationship' between outcomes and subsequent actions as suggesting that 'TAP's early development may have largely consisted of escalating commitments to failing courses of action' (as observed by Argyris and Schön 1978 and by Ross and Staw 1986).

In the contraction period, the authors do see evidence of adaptive, trial-and-error learning. They observe that entrepreneurs showed a propensity 'to select the course of action that was rewarded,' whereas negative outcomes 'triggered interventions by resource controllers, which resulted in changes in the innovation unit's course of action' (1992: 104). These changes led, in turn, to shifts in outcome criteria, suggesting to the authors that 'outcome criteria may have shifted largely to justify changes' in the course of action.

The authors' findings lead them to pose three puzzling questions:

1. Why did trial-and-error learning not occur during TAP's expansion period?

2. What explains the dramatic shift from little or no learning during the expansion period to trial-and-error learning during TAP's contraction period?

3. When learning occurred, it appeared too late. Why was TAP's development terminated (1992: 106)?

The Behavioral Story

It is in their exploration of these puzzles that the authors turn to the phenomena they call 'behavioral'. They observe that during the expansion phase the innovation entrepreneurs were held accountable for achieving the overly optimistic plans they had presented in order to secure funding. This, in turn, triggered 'sugar-coated' administrative reviews. None of managers of the innovation team interviewed by the authors showed a willingness to 'document uncertainties or to propose a more extended timetable for start-up, because they feared that would decrease their chances of obtaining start-up funding'. The top managers of the parent companies that funded TAP accepted the overoptimistic planning targets presented by the entrepreneurs, although they admitted privately that 'they discounted certain projections as "fluff" and expected the plan to change'. Nevertheless, they held publicly to the conviction that TAP managers should be kept accountable to their plans. This, in turn, 'precipitated *the onset of a vicious cycle of impression management* between innovation managers and resource controllers' (1992: 106; emphasis added).

While development efforts were largely successful in this period, they did encounter critical difficulties—for example, manufacturing defects and problems in scaling up production of the filtration module—which resulted in slipped marketing schedules, deferred sales revenues, and delayed development of the Phase H device (1992: 106). During the administrative review sessions that were held every six months or so the TAP managers reported information about these problems to the resource controllers, but they did so in ways that were calculated to discourage problem solving and learning. Van de Ven and Polley (1992: 107) report that before each review session the TAP managers spent a day

rehearsing their presentations, developing tactics and scripts on how they would respond to possible questions of top managers...preparing 'slick' visuals... and [reconstructing] negative information in a positive frame, with assurances that they were in control of problems and presented action plans for addressing [them]... The resource controllers... relied on this indirect information to assess TAP's progress... and tended to mimic the TAP success criteria and concerns they were told by innovation managers.

In the expansion phase, setbacks occurred frequently, and red flags were raised with increasing frequency concerning TAP's development, schedule, directions, and financing. Nevertheless, the authors observed relatively few attempts to 'detect these warnings as errors and correct the detected errors'. Some warnings provoked discussion and debate, but most 'were simply aired without response or were dismissed as irrelevant'. At no time in the expansion period did TAP managers 'seriously question the assumptions or validity of the technological paths they were pursuing' (1992: 108).

The authors account for these remarkable (though classic) findings by reference to two main factors, in addition to vicious circles of impression management. First, a high level of discontinuity in the TAP personnel, due to normal job mobility and promotion in the parent companies, disrupted the continuity of attention necessary for adaptive learning. Second, the proliferation of 'parallel and independent streams of research activities' appeared to have the effect of '[masking] attention to the core innovation idea: the viability of producing a single reliable filtration device' (1992: 107). They suggest that this noise, which went far beyond the information-processing capacity of individuals, makes it easy to understand 'why so few messages were detected as errors' and 'why few attempts were observed to correct detected errors' (1992: 110).

In the contraction phase, things changed. First of all, TAP got into serious trouble when its managers tried to introduce the Phase I devices into the European market and use them to conduct clinical trials of the Phase II filtration module. Even so, the authors report, the negative assessment of TAP's performance did not begin to grow until it was revealed at an administrative review session that development targets for the Phase II device had slipped by over a year and that sales revenues from the Phase I device were at 10 per cent of projections. Only then did resource controllers begin to raise serious questions about TAP's development and intervene to break the pattern of persisting in failing courses of action. At this point the resource controllers put new TAP managers in charge of manufacturing. These managers suspended all shipments of Phase I devices and conducted an extensive internal review and audit of the scale-up and manufacturing problems; as a result several TAP people were laid off. As one member of the TAP unit observed at the time, 'My honeymoon is over' (1992: 112).

These events produced what the authors regard as a further cause of increased adaptive learning, that is, a concentration of attention on pressing operational problems, which had the effect of 'reducing complexity and focusing attention on a single issue', which, in turn, 'facilitated trial-and-error learning' (1992: 110). Sophisticated technological and engineering trials and adaptations were made, and long-standing manufacturing defects were finally corrected. As a result, the TAP device was found to achieve 'a reliability rate comparable to competing apheresis devices in the market' (1992: 112).

Nevertheless, the troubles experienced in this phase shook the resource controllers' confidence. They began to pay serious attention to the mounting development costs that were draining resources from alternative investments. In contrast, the innovation managers saw the recent setbacks as temporary and maintained their long-term commitment to the program (1992: 112). The two parties developed 'alternative stories that interpreted the same experience quite differently'. Meanwhile, in the external environment 'latent forces' were gathering. In the parent companies, budgets were being reduced in the face of negative corporate earnings. A CEO who had been one of TAP's principal supporters died unexpectedly. There was news of technological advances by TAP's Japanese competitors and rumors that a new drug might do away with the need for apheresis hardware. Then, when it became evident that development targets had slipped by over a year and that market trials had revealed serious manufacturing defects, these latent forces were unleashed. In November 1988, TAP was terminated.

In reality, the authors point out, there were fewer threatening events during the contraction period than in the expansion period, but TAP had lost its credibility. The resource controllers launched a search for a new corporate investor, and, finding none, they declared TAP a failure. Was it a failure? The authors end their story by quoting a senior executive in one of TAP's parent organizations: had the program been allowed to continue, he thought, it might have succeeded.

The TAP Analysis Analyzed

As an account of a technological innovation, the TAP story has a familiar ring (see, for example, Schön 1967). Throughout the early stages of the process, researchers and general managers pursue a game of reciprocal deception and attempted unilateral control: researchers smooth over negative information and general managers delay attending to negative signals. This goes on until a crisis occurs, at which point the researchers can no longer mask the negative information, managers can no longer avoid paying attention to it, and they overreact.

At the very end of their version of this classic story, the authors (1992: 114–15) suggest some things organizations can do to enhance the prospects for adaptive learning.

1. Separate the planning from the funding of a new venture, so as to avoid optimistic estimates aimed mainly at securing funding.
2. Find ways to decrease the bull index, that is, the high amount of impression management that goes on between innovation teams and investors and distorts information needed for trial-and-error learning.
3. Keep the core innovation team intact during innovation development.

4. Keep innovation development and business creation separate, so as to reduce information overload.
5. 'Alter the agendas and formats of...administrative review sessions in order to increase the amount of candid information exchange and learning'.

What is striking about Van de Ven and Polley's treatment of the TAP story is that they are very rigorous in their testing of the adaptive learning model, yet they make so little explanatory use of their behavioral data. The mixed results of their test of the adaptive learning model lead to important puzzles:

- Why was adaptive learning so long delayed?
- Why was there a dramatic shift to adaptive learning in the contraction phase?
- Why, when adaptive learning finally occurred, did controllers pull the plug?

In their use of the behavioral story to resolve these puzzles, the authors note the ambiguous information, the shifting objectives, and the uncertainties surrounding the development, complexity and noise in the information environment, and the discontinuities of personnel. They treat these explanations as partial causes of the lack of adaptive learning in the expansion phase.

But such phenomena are the givens of research and development programs. All such programs encounter them in greater or lesser degree. The key question is: how and through what kinds of interpersonal inquiry participants in a development deal with such phenomena? Given the uncertainties inherent in a development project, do the participants seek to make public their doubts as well as their beliefs? Do they invite challenges to their positions or expose the dilemmas with which they themselves are struggling? Given endemic noise, ambiguity, and uncertainty, do they seek out and invite public testing of assumptions that underlie the core innovation idea? Or do they enter into a vicious circle of impression management, as in the TAP story, with innovation managers suppressing uncertainties and smoothing over negative information in order to keep the controllers from taking setbacks seriously and with controllers colluding with the researchers by holding them publicly to overoptimistic targets whose 'fluff' they privately acknowledge?

The authors note these features of organizational inquiry, which they express at relatively high levels on the ladder of inference ('sugar coating', 'impression management'), but they offer no coherent theory to explain them. From my point of view, the participants' vicious circles of impression management are predictable variants of primary inhibitory loops, triggered by the threat or embarrassment associated with situations of uncertainty and ambiguity. In these collusive processes, both parties employ a Model I strategy of mystery and mastery. They keep mysterious what they know to be true (the fluffy estimates, the likelihood that plans will change), while outwardly they try to master the responses of the other party. Under these conditions, errors and setbacks in the development's trajectory and uncertainties about its future cannot be made public; to do so would reveal both parties' deceptions. So the crucially important errors and uncertainties along with their undiscussability are kept undiscussable, until a critical event (the flawed entry into the European market, for example) makes error unavoidably visible, provoking a crisis that triggers the resource managers' precipitate termination of the project.

Such a vicious circle is explicable, indeed predictable, on the basis of Model I theories-in-use, which shape interpersonal inquiry under conditions of threat or embarrassment. These theories-in-use reinforce and are, in turn, reinforced by the organizational learning systems. As we see it, this is the systematic explanation of the patterns of unreliable organizational inquiry through which the actors in the TAP story respond to uncertainty, complexity, ambiguity, and discontinuity—the givens of technological entrepreneurship. From this viewpoint, one sees the flimsiness of the authors' prescriptions for enhancing adaptive learning. How will the separation of planning from funding decisions encourage adaptive learning if, once the funds are granted, the innovation team persists in its strategies of control through deception, and the resource controllers collude in appearing to swallow such deceptions in order to control the researchers by holding them publicly to their formal targets? How will the participants reduce the 'bull index' when their theories-in use lead them to produce and accept the bull? How will altering agendas and formats lead to an increase in candid information exchange and learning when such candidness would threaten to surface data that both parties actively work at keeping undiscussable?

The patterns of behavior implicit in the vicious circle of impression management are unlikely to change unless the participants invite an intervention that creates the conditions for the kind of 'open, fact-based conversation' that Van de Ven and Polley recommend, or unless the participants learn to develop Model II theories-in-use, as we have illustrated earlier, so as to create such conditions for themselves. Model II action strategies—for example, the public testing of privately held assumptions and attributions—do not require a prior removal of conditions of ambiguity and uncertainty. On the contrary, it is precisely under profound uncertainty and ambiguity, when one cannot know what the truth is, that Model II inquiry is most needed and most likely to create the conditions for good dialectic.

Whether or not readers accept the analysis of the behavioral phenomena described in the TAP story, I hope it is now clear why such phenomena must be considered characteristically organizational and crucially linked to organizational learning. Consider the following propositions arrayed in descending order on a ladder of aggregation:

1. In the expansion phase of the TAP project, there was an organizational failure of adaptive learning.
2. In their administrative reviews during this phase, innovation managers and resource controllers engaged in a vicious circle of impression management.
3. In any given instance of such a review, an innovation manager, A, gave a 'sugar-coated' account of progress, knowing

that he was doing so but keeping that knowledge to himself; and a resource controller, B, privately discounted that statement as 'fluff' but kept that knowledge to himself.

If, following Van de Ven and Polley, we treat item 1 as a proposition about organizational phenomena and item 2 as a partial explanation of item 1, how then can we not also treat item 2 as about organizational phenomena? And if we treat item 3 as a specification and partial explanation of item 2, then how are we justified in excluding it from the set of propositions that refer to organizational phenomena? We cannot validly exclude from the class of propositions about organizations those that offer explanations of phenomena that we already treat as organizational. More specifically, we cannot validly exclude from the class of propositions about organizational learning those propositions about interpersonal inquiry in organizations that are adduced to explain observed patterns of organizational learning.

If this argument holds for the explanation of organizational learning, it holds all the more so for prescriptions aimed at enhancing it. Practitioners will be unable to act on such prescriptions unless they already have the skills required to carry out the actions prescribed.

They will not be able to enact a prescription such as 'Cut the bull index' ' or 'Hold candid, fact-based conversations' unless the prescription is formulated in terms that enable them to envisage actions required for its implementation.

SUMMARY

Errors are mismatches between intended outcomes and actual outcomes. The intended outcomes are espoused theories of action. The actual outcomes are produced by master programs such as theories-in-use and their component sub-routines called designs-in-use.

The actual outcomes illustrated in the two cases discussed in this chapter are actions produced by Model I theories-in-use and the organizational defensive routines at all levels of the organization: run silent–run deep are consistent with Model I and organizational defensive routines. The same may be said of the political games played by the TAP group *and* those played by the top management when it recognized the games and acted as if they did not exist. It took a massive failure that could no longer lie hidden to expose the gaming. Yet even then the games continued because the product innovation was cancelled by top management citing reasons that did not include the gaming.

The gamings produced are illicit in terms of formal management practices in both organizations. In order to produce them, it is also necessary to produce cover-ups and to cover up the cover-ups.

These designed errors are produced by using a theory-in-use that is organizationally illicit. In the minds of the producers, designed errors are necessary for the achievement of organizational goals (for example, produce micro-processors) and for individual survival (run silent, run deep). Also, in the minds of producers the acknowledgement of such a strategy is foolhardy. The designed error is therefore a mismatch between action and organizational requirements produced by design-in-use, that is, in effect, a match. A designed error is a second-order error. At the second order it is a mismatch.

Under these conditions, the participants know that they are playing games whose rules are: I know that I am and you are covering up. You know the same about me. Both of us know that we will not make what we know discussable. Both of us know that we will act as if we are not playing this game.

There is an ethical double-bind embedded in these games. On the one hand, the players collude to cover up in the name of caring and concern for others and for the organization. On the other hand, they promise to show integrity by not exposing the games. One wonders if such games are not involved in creating 'slippery slopes' for human beings to go along with unethical actions. Perhaps the debacles described in Chapter 1—Enron, Arthur Anderson, FBI, CIA, Catholic Church, and public school teachers—were informed by such defensive theories-in-use.

To extend the conjecture, those involved know that their actions are questionable. They learn to live with this designed dishonesty by convincing themselves they have no choice; they are victims of the double bind that is sanctioned by Model I organizational defenses. One consequence of being a victim is to distance oneself from one's personal causal responsibility in creating and colluding with this predicament.

This analysis provides credibility to Professor Burgelman's claim that that significant changes to these defensive routines are unlikely. My inference is that the analysis, one hopes, increases our realization that empirical research is needed that may provide new strategies that liberate us from defensive double binds.

4

Inhibiting Double-Loop Learning in Government and Information Technology

The problems described in Chapter 3 are generalizable to other contexts. I begin with a selected review of the literature on governmental organizations. I then take a different cut and review selected literature on information technology (IT) representing corporations, governmental agencies, and not-for-profit organizations. Finally I will examine some research on knowledge management. The researchers claim that they are able to produce double-loop learning; however, my examination casts doubts on this claim. But it serves a useful purpose by showing how single-loop and double-loop learning differ.

GOVERNMENTAL ORGANIZATIONS

Halperin (1974) writes that pet projects and defensive games in governmental organizations are almost never made explicit but are nonetheless well-understood by the participants, that personal challenges are often wrapped in substantive guise, that people may take the opposite stance to the one they prefer if their preferred stance is seen as deviant, and that people accept such rules as necessary in order to survive.

Etheredge (1985) details blocks to learning that occurred during crucial decision-making governmental meetings. The blocks included lying or deception within the executive branch; engaging in politically sophisticated behavior that produced a system that moved increasingly further from reality; ignoring orders and cutting corners, thereby keeping the President ignorant of reality; accepting neither bureaucratic nor personal responsibility; and holding ritualized meetings that discouraged re-examination and rethinking. Etheredge (1985: 161) suggests that these games are characteristic of competitive, power-oriented individuals who enjoy playing hardball politics. Brunsson (1989: 58), in a study of Swedish local authorities, reports that actors would agree that they had failed and that they could not justify their behavior, but 'although they knew they were doing the wrong thing, they went on doing it'. He describes behavior patterns in which local authorities 'administer' problems in ways that inhibit the changes they admit are desired (1989: 68), yet they see no way out. These patterns, they suggest, are in the nature of politics.

Kaufman (1981) describes how White House staff dealt with their fears of agencies becoming too independent by increasing controls. The agencies responded by complaining and by trying to bypass the controls, but the White House then further increased the control. This created self-reinforcing, self-sealing processes with a life of their own.

A similar process appears in the report of the Rogers Commission, which investigated the disaster of the loss of the space shuttle Challenger. The Commission determined that

safety was inexplicably poorly dealt with given the attention, personnel, and commitment the participants had to the subject. A disastrous situation was developing. While NASA and the others were capable of recognizing the problem and reporting it, the relevant players did not do so. The 'can-do' attitude at all levels of the task at hand led everyone to focus on operational objectives. Once the focus was on getting the shuttle launched, the attention of the participants was diverted.   (Presidential Commission 1986: 56)

The Commission recommended strengthening the emphasis on safety by adding new roles with power to deal with safety and new rules to make sure safety was not ignored. The implication was that a Czar for safety and new control procedures would solve the problems. What was not focused upon was why safety was handled in a poor way in an organization that understood the importance of safety.

David Stockman's White House education and disillusionment as director of the Office of Management and Budget began with the early meetings of the President and the cabinet (Stockman 1986a). Often, the President did not understand the essence of the argument. Even more often, Edwin Meese (counselor to the President) would manage the meetings so that no thorough airing of views was possible, and actions like these were not discussable.

Stockman and his associates decided on several bypass strategies. For example, Stockman (1986a: 102) reports, they learned to generate non-controversial ideas for discussion during the meetings: 'We had to scramble all week to find enough of these "safe" items to fill Meese's Cabinet agenda while "big ticket" spending cuts and economic forecast items receded further and further'. Stockman concluded that the tough decisions were not going to be made in the cabinet meetings 'because Ed Meese was protecting the President from having to choose sides among his Cabinet members' (1986a: 109). Stockman had to devise a bypass strategy that would work over time but would not be viewed as a means to bypass Meese's and others' protection of the President's and cabinet members' intellectual and interpersonal limits. Stockman hit on a structural solution often used by individuals in this predicament.

Stockman proposed to Meese that he create a committee called the Budget Working Group, which would review all budget cuts with affected cabinet members before the cuts went to the President and the full cabinet. Even though Meese and Chief of Staff James Baker would be members of the group, Stockman knew that neither of them would attend the meetings unless the President did. Meese agreed, and Stockman selected his team. It was this group that made most of the difficult choices.

The Budget Working Group meetings also became the setting for Stockman and his associate Martin Anderson, a policy analyst, to educate new cabinet members and their staffs about the rigors of budget cutting. Anderson, says Stockman, knew how to cut the resisters down to size without humiliating them. Stockman does not describe exactly how Anderson accomplished this feat. People can sense when they are being cut down to size and when the cutting down is being covered up. They play along by covering up their humiliation and anger. These bad feelings accumulate, however, and soon these people find appropriate ways to retaliate.

Stockman's descriptions suggest that humiliation and anger may have been present and that retaliation did occur. He notes that the cabinet members and their staffs began to resist. He also overheard cabinet members talking with each other about his heavy-handedness. Moreover, cabinet members and their staffs developed their own defensive actions. Secretary of Defense Caspar Weinberger and Secretary of the Treasury Donald Regan were especially skillful here.

On reflection, Stockman admits it could appear that cabinet members acted irresponsibly, sweeping issues under the rug and basing short-run policy and political gains on weak facts (Stockman 1986b: 14). But the actors, Stockman insists, were not clearly aware of their own actions: 'I don't think anybody lied... [There was] no deliberate deception... we were confused... but nobody said, "we know we're lying, but we're going to go ahead and do it anyway"... And we were all caught up in those daily tactical battles... we never had time to raise... the big picture doubts' (1986b: 15–6).

What can we infer from these examples about the way governmental agencies are administered? The immediate impact of the policies, practices, and behavior described in the literature was to inhibit the detection and correction of error. The second-order consequence was to inhibit problem solving and decision-making. This consequence led to a third-order consequence: less effective organizational performance.

In addition, all the actions occurred where a wide variety of issues were being dealt with. The issues were complex and non-trivial, and they contained a potential for, or an actual component of, embarrassment or threat. Moreover, the embarrassment or threat could be aimed at individuals, groups, intergroups, or whole organizations. All this is consistent with the impact of Model I theory-in-use and organizational defensive routines.

Turning to the advice on how to deal with these issues, the authors do not focus on the causes of the patterns that they reported. This results in advice that has low implementable validity. For example, Halperin (1974) recommends that the President of the United States deal with people's games and defenses by advantageous bargaining. According to Halperin, one of the President's most powerful assets is his ability to persuade associates that something he wishes to do is in the national interest. People take him seriously when he believes his ideas personally and evokes national interest. When this does not work, he negotiates. And if this is not adequate, he may bully. Finally, he may simply take over as much of the execution as possible. The President may also fire certain players and bring in new ones.

It is not clear, however, how any of these tactics would engage, overcome, and reduce organizational defensive routines. Indeed, as I read Halperin's recommendations, it is almost as if the defenses did not exist in his situation—or, if they did, were not important. Clearly, Halperin's book documents that they did exist and that they were important.

Kaufman (1977) identifies three solutions to stronger control: reduce the size of government, strengthen controls, and provide incentives to private interests to do what the government is doing. After assessing the advantages and disadvantages of the solutions, Kaufman recommends that the government should treat symptoms, because they will relieve pain; have appeal processes that work; provide citizens with help, so that rules are not seen as barriers; and provide an ombudsman. But he does not say what specific actions are required to treat symptoms effectively, create appeal processes that work, or give help that actually overcomes the barriers. Again, the advice is abstract; it bypasses the very dysfunctional processes that Kaufman describes, and he himself finally concludes that we may have to live with a little red tape because that is the nature of the beast.

Wilson (1989: 396–72) suggests that, in order for bureaucracies to become more effective, there should be more deregulation, executives who understand their organizational cultures, negotiations to identify essential and non-essential constraints, authority pushed down to the lowest possible levels, judgements based on results, and clear standard operating procedures. However, these recommendations also fail to deal with organizational defensive routines.

The same problem occurs with Janis's (1972) recommendations for overcoming 'group think'. For example, having someone play devil's advocate is unlikely to reduce defensive routines, as Secretary George Ball found out during the Vietnam war era. Nor is Bardach and Kagan's recommendation (1982) to impose budget constraints on regulatory unreasonableness likely to induce reason.

The literature on leadership in government is no more helpful (see Burns 1978; Barber 1977; Gardner 1990; Paige 1977; McFarland 1969; and the contributors to Kellerman 1984). Burns speaks of transformational leadership at such an abstract level that it is difficult to see how that quality could be learned from his discussion, which omits important behavioral puzzles and dilemmas. For example, Bailey (1988) describes Roosevelt as designedly playing one subordinate against another. Edelman (1988) also describes Roosevelt as being skillful in acting deceptively and manipulating people. Yet Burns describes Roosevelt as a transformational leader. According to Edelman, John Kennedy, Lyndon Johnson, and Richard Nixon also acted inconsistently and deceptively. The actions mentioned are all consistent with the organizational defenses described earlier, and it may well be that transformational leaders succeed partially by being deceptive, but one would not know that from the research literature on leadership.

Two recommendations appear to have the potential to genuinely reduce the likelihood of embarrassment or threat. However, to my knowledge, neither strategy has been studied empirically to assess its practical strengths and weaknesses.

The first strategy—a strategy of group deliberation and decision-making—is recommended by George (1972) as a way to develop more valid information and dialogue for the President regarding foreign policy. However, he supplies no discussion or research on how his strategy would work if the issues were threatening or embarrassing to the players. Perhaps the moment defensive routines become activated, the effectiveness of the structural arrangements suggested would be significantly limited.

The second strategy, recommended by Neustadt and May (1986), suggests that actors examine their presumptions rigorously when reaching decisions about important issues. Neustadt and May show that some important errors in Vietnam war policy might have been averted if government officials had probed their own presumptions. Again, research is required to see how the reasonableness of this method might be sabotaged when individual, group, and organizational defenses are activated.

I should like to extend this line of reasoning by using a different set of data collected during some experiments while teaching a course (with Professor Lawrence Lynn, who was then at Kennedy School of Government, in August 1985). The data showed that the same gaps and inconsistencies found in the advice in the literature cited above can be replicated in classrooms composed of civil servants.

The study was conducted during three different years. There were two classes each year. Each class was composed of about 100 students from government organizations representing different roles, ages, genders, and organizational position. The students were asked to evaluate the effectiveness of the actions of two competing groups charged with defining welfare policy during President Jimmy Carter's administration. The students read the same case describing the relevant events (Lynn and Whiteman 1981).

The case served as a projective technique. The students used it to project their views and attitudes based on their experiences as civil servants.

If governmental organizations were composed of individuals using Model I and organizational defensive routines, then an analysis of their diagnostic actions in class should be consistent with these features. The students should not act in ways that are consistent with Model II theory-in-use. A hearing of the tape recordings of each class produced the analysis below. The illustrations are shortened versions of their conversations.

The students' diagnosis of the action in the case began with their analysis of the working groups. These were described as two groups that:

- had entrenched positions;
- were unwilling to change;
- had lots of disagreement;
- were miscommunicating;
- were not accustomed to working with each other;
- had no one confronting the real issues;
- had delegates from Moscow;
- pushed their own agendas any time they could do so.

Secretary of Health, Education, and Welfare Joseph Califano was 'Washington-hip':

- He let things boil.
- He kept options open.
- He was smart enough to know that if he accepted responsibility, he also would get all the trouble.
- He appeared to have a secret agenda.

Vintage Califano behavior was that he had learned to humiliate his staff from Lyndon Johnson, he acted like a trial lawyer, he acted bored in order to collect his thoughts.

- The deadline placed people under pressure.
- No one was willing to make firm decisions. Each player thought 'It is not my decision to make'.
- This is the dynamic of the first six months of any administration. The players are finding their way around, jockeying for position. Turf is being defined.
- Califano did not know his staff. They were afraid to level with him. They told him what they thought he wanted to hear.

- The groups had the typical Washington mentality: throw money at problems and take care of constituents.
- Everyone was acting rationally—each group felt it had the answer and acted as if it did. It is rational to resist (carefully and adroitly) giving up one's position. Hence, Carter might have been able to push a button and launch a missile, but he pushed Califano and nothing got done.
- There was an underlying tension between the Georgia hicks and the Washington sophisticates.

The members of the second session repeated the causes the first session had described and added some further ones:

1. The task itself contained conflicting features: on the one hand, redesign welfare; on the other hand, add no more cost, in order to keep inflation down.
2. The situation set up a classic power struggle. Why do we expect anything but what happened? Why are we surprised? The players were heads of agencies and were born winners, ambitious men who wanted to win. If they lost, they would lose the respect of their staffs.
3. The players were selfish and self-centered, looking out for number one, obsessed with maintaining 'my truth'. People's self-esteem is wrapped up in game-playing and they are afraid to say they do not know what to do.
4. None of the players had a great vision, an important organizing idea about welfare.
   No one really seemed to care about welfare reform.
   We lack mature leaders; there is no one with wisdom.
   We have dropped the 'philosopher' from 'philosopher–prince'.
5. Each institution was self-centered, with its own learning experiences and perspective; none wished to cooperate.
6. The task was too large to do all at once. It might have worked out if done incrementally.

The participants in both sessions judged the actors in the case of welfare reform to be largely ineffective. An examination of the talk crafted by the students in the classes indicates the following. First, the responses represented unillustrated, untested attributions or evaluations, advocacy of participants' views with little encouragement or inquiry by others, and attributions that place the responsibility 'in' individuals or in cultural forces. These are all defensive routines.

Second, the diagnoses contain an implicit causal theory of effectiveness that may be stated as follows: if individuals or groups use untested attributions, advocacy that curtails inquiry, and attributions that assign responsibility to individuals or cultural forces, the individuals or groups will harden their positions, develop rivalries, become mistrustful, and distance themselves from taking the responsibility for confronting process issues. These outcomes, in turn, will lead to escalating error, undiscussability of the counterproductive features in the settings where they are occurring (but discussability among friends or cliques), and players who act as if there were nothing undiscussable (one cannot discuss the undiscussability of the undiscussable).

Moreover, if the actors in the Califano case had asked the class to evaluate their effectiveness, and if the class had stated these causal views directly, the class would have been using the same counterproductive behavior, the same kinds of attributing and advocating that they condemned the actors in the case for using. In other words, if the Califano players had listened to the class dialogue, they would probably have become defensive.

During the class discussion, a number of opportunities arose to illustrate this hypothesis. Frequently, a faculty member would ask the class how they would communicate to the actors in the case what the students were saying about them in class. Almost always, the students would try to ease in to the criticism. In the few instances when students were forthright, many of the class members laughed. When asked why, they answered that it was unrealistic to think that one could be forthright with the President, Califano, and the other major actors.

To summarize, the students diagnosed the players' actions in the case as defensive, but the very way they framed their diagnoses would also have created defensiveness if the players had heard them. During the class, the students created defensiveness in each other when they disagreed. The point is that the defensive behavior was so skilled and automatic that the students behaved in the very ways they condemned the players for behaving. In addition, the students were unaware of their defensiveness, and most said that they would never have predicted that they would act as they did.

INFORMATION TECHNOLOGY

The[1] claim that low trust, politicizing, and organizational defensive routines are counterproductive to effective implementation is also prevalent in the IT literature. So is the systematic bypassing of what can be done to reduce the counterproductive consequences. Where advice is provided, it is abstract and provides no prescriptive designs for the human mind to make it actionable.

For example, Sproull and Keisler (1991) report that individuals should learn to act more caringly and supportively in ways that are more effective than the traditional (read Model I) ones. The readers may understand the advice. The problem is that the only theory-in-use they have is Model I. Moreover, since human beings programmed with Model I are not effective at detecting and correcting their errors, and since if they detect errors they have learned to blame others, the advice implemented will not be the one that is intended. And the players will be unaware of this possibility.

Norman (1998) recommends that development teams should be close-knit and its members open to confronting each other constructively. But what happens if genuine attention to the task produces embarrassment or threat? Norman does not provide theory-in-use advice.

Trust is rare yet key to effective implementation. It is best created through face-to-face contacts. In these contacts, trust must be visible, ubiquitous, and start at the top (Davenport and Prusak

---

[1] For a different but informative perspective on IT, see Ciborra (2001; 2002).

1998; Rockart, Earl, and Ross 1996). How are these features to be produced by human beings programmed with Model I, skilled at producing mistrust, and all this reinforced by organizational defenses?

Avisin and Wood-Harper (1990) report that effective implementation is impeded by organizational politics, protecting one's turf, and the different perspectives of the professionals involved. The authors do not specify how to bring about change. Other authors are more explicit as to actions that may be taken to assure effective implementation. For example, Norman (1998) recommends that they tell the people that they will not tolerate resistance. This is consistent with Model I at best, and assures external commitment.

O'Dell and Grayson (1998) recommend the use of internal benchmarking, mapping the knowledge, and capturing and summarizing lessons learned. The problem not addressed is that the existing organizational defensive routines and the accompanying defensive reasoning can reduce the validity of such actions and, of course, cover up such barriers.

Mendelson and Ziegler (1999) recommend that organizations learn to listen to customers and non-customers, especially to those who may be disappointed and angry. Implementing such advice is fraught with embarrassment or threat, especially if it has not been accepted as valid in the past. The authors do not help us to see how the Model I skilled incompetence and unawareness are to be overcome. Mendelson and Ziegler (1999) also describe successful organizations as emphasizing local authority, initiative, participation, and empowerment. Again, these espoused descriptions are disconnected from actual behavior.

A second problem is that the causal actions to produce the positive consequences described by the authors are not made transparent. For example, external information awareness causes a sense of urgency. Everyone must internalize the fact that time is crucial. Precisely how does awareness of external information produce a sense of urgency? What kind of internalization, and how is it created?

The authors suggest that communicating evidence of success in other organizations helps. But data show that such evidence may not create a sense of internalized urgency. If urgency exists, it is largely externally produced. The authors also advise such practices as no-excuse analysis. Again, these may be especially successful with some executives and in some organizations but not with others (Argyris 1990a; Argyris and Kaplan 1994).

The real problem is that these gaps and inconsistencies produce and reinforce organizational defensive routines. These defensive routines, in turn, influence negatively the production of valid information and strengthen bypass, cover-up, and undiscussability. All these consequences inhibit effective management of information. It may well be that none of these consequences occurred in the organizations the authors described. Unfortunately, the authors do not provide the behavioral data required to permit the readers to make up their own minds.

The firm of the future, Teece (1998) advises, will focus heavily on its ability to create, transfer, assemble, integrate, and exploit knowledge assets. The emphasis will be more on the entrepreneurial than the administrative side of corporate governance. The causal basis for sensing and responding is the increasingly sophisticated information technology that is able to map the new complexity faced by executives with accuracy, speed, and transparency. It is this information technology that will overcome the fundamental barrier to effective management, namely, bounded rationality.

This causal claim, I suggest, is valid but incomplete. The limit of information-processing capabilities is only one of three barriers. The other two are Model I theories-in-use and organizational defensive routines. They act to limit the effective use of knowledge by systematically blinding the users to recognizing, producing, and implementing valid information. Moreover, they make the skillful incompetence and unawareness undiscussable and the undiscussability undiscussable. Teece, like other scholars cited above, recognizes that a key, if not *the* key, medium for communicating knowledge is face-to-face relationships. This is precisely where Model I theories-in-use and organizational defensive routines have their most powerful impact.

GAMING THE SYSTEM

Organizations are increasingly creating an underground system of knowledge that is intended to protect its players at all levels of the organization. Not surprisingly, covering up its existence protects an underground system.

For example, a divisional president resisted the advice of his immediate subordinates to game their presentation to the CEO because they feared that a valid presentation could close down the division or attach it to other existing organizations. The divisional president argued that the results should not be distorted. Moreover, he promised that, if they made a sound presentation, it would lead top management to permit them to design how to implement the recommendations.

The presentation was a success and the CEO did order the changes that the divisional subordinates feared. The divisional president admitted that he had lost the control that he had promised. When he returned to his group, he admitted his disappointment. He then added that he and others had learned not to be so naive the next time. Games of survival may have to be played.

Golding (1991) describes the 'rituals' (routines) in an organization that restricted the flow of relevant financial information to the top level. Other managers who tried to get the information they needed concluded it was a waste of time to try. They also concluded that the meetings they attended were a waste of time, but they continued to attend them, covering up their true feelings. Golding also describes rituals to cover up secrecy. He concludes that many of this organization's rituals produced status degradation and intimidation to the point of becoming oppressive; but he also concludes, as I understand it, that these rituals will continue. He suggests that trying to stop these rituals would be as futile as trying to, as he puts it, stop the clock. Ironically, studies such as this make it less likely that social science research will be able to stop the clock by changing the status quo. Golding, in my opinion, describes the defensive reality of the organization accurately. But, by stopping there and not conducting research on changing the rituals, he provides both the researchers who document oppressive routines and the executives who produce them with an explanation that permits them to conclude that their defensive routines cannot be changed.

As researchers, I suggest, we have a responsibility to try to change defensive routines in order to develop empirical knowledge about their alterability. At the moment, because of the absence of such studies coupled with the large number of studies describing organizational defensive routines, we may be encouraging scholars and practitioners to believe that the status quo, and its errors and defensive routines, is unalterable.

Benssaon and Earl (1998) have reported that Japanese firms may have less gaming of IT and other organizational problems because IT focuses less on the strategic issues and more on the operational routine issues. To the extent the operational issues are routine, less complex, and less threatening, one can predict that there will be less gaming. However, even in this domain Benssaon and Earl[2] found some degree of anxiety on the part of those who felt that even the more operational uses of IT may lead to their loss of control. It may be that one way to reduce gaming is to give effective IT systems the features of information appliance, namely, simplicity, versatility, and pleasurability. A toaster is an example. The complexity required to achieve the task is built into the toaster. The user is left with very few actions to perform (Norman 1998). This strategy is easily monitored because it is transparent. Hedberg et al. (1997) suggest these features will make the implementability of IT more effective.

Lucas (1981) and Lucas, Ginzberg, and Schultz (1990) do focus on the importance of human variables, but largely at the level of espoused theory that produces altruist advice. Malone (1997) and

---

[2] Personal communication.

Malone *et al.* (1997) warn that the pay-off of IT can be limited by such factors as trust, personal motivations, distribution of power, and personalities. They do not specify the actions required to produce these features.

MORE USER-FRIENDLY COMPUTERS

In closing, I should like to examine the research on creating a 'fit' between the computer and the user. Those who wish to increase the degree of user friendliness must realize, the advisers say, that the relationship is an interpersonal one. In the eyes of the users, the interface has personality characteristics. Human beings automatically and often unconsciously apply social rules to their interactions with computers. More attention should be paid to these rules to make computers more user-friendly (Friedman 1997; Nass *et al.* 1997). The authors report that users often conceive of computer programs as having a personality feature such as being dominant. Some users prefer this computer personality; many do not. If computer programs were designed to create a better fit, they would be more user-friendly.

Another finding is that a better fit should be designed between social rules such as politeness norms, flattery, and gender stereotypes. Users report more positive feelings if the computer takes into account such social rules.

Nardi and O'Day (1999) report a similar set of results. Information technology was found to be more user-friendly when it took into account social rules of the local setting. For example, a user framed a question for a librarian. The librarian realized the framing was incorrect. The librarian reframed the question so that the user would get the information requested. In the interest of being diplomatic and caring, the reframing was done covertly. The user, unaware of the reframing, left happy and pleased.

In another example, a computer program was designed to 'gag' those who dominated the conversation and enhanced defensive dialogue and to do so without making the feature transparent (which could escalate the defensiveness). This may be user-friendly but it may be achieving these features at a hidden but fundamental cost. First, politeness norms, diplomacy, flattery, and gag rules require that these intentions be covered up. In order for any cover-up to work, it too must be covered up. User-friendly advice such as this teaches social rules that inhibit transparency and genuine testing of the impact of such actions.

Creating a fit between the personality of the computer program and the user may make the user feel better. But one reason that the user feels better is that the 'fit' does not require that he or she examine the basis for the personality preference. For example, we have found that a preference for domination or passivity may be based on self-protection. Self-protection, in turn, predisposes individuals to be blind to the learning they should get if they are to be effective. If we want to support learning, then a minimal fit may be important if it is accompanied by a program to learn from the lack of fit. Recall the example of the 'gag' program. The users rejected its use because they did not consider it an effective way to deal with conflict. Apparently, the computer professionals did not produce a program that would help users learn how to deal more effectively with conflict.

The literature cautions IT professionals that there is a disjunction between the theory of design and implementation they hold and what it means to be human. For example, computer programs are deterministic (Holland 1993; Norman 1998; Landon and Landon 1998; Danziger and Kraemer 1986; Galliers and Baets 1998). Computers are limited by their particular emphasis on technical methods (Introna and Whitley 1997) and their dedication to focus on completeness and objectivity (Bloomfield and Vurdubakes 1997). These features are valid. The problem arises when the IT programs are implemented in organizations. Model I theory-in-use organizational defensive routines are then activated. These features have their own 'method-ism', their own views of completeness and objectivity. They combine to create their own ultra-stable states with their own determinism and its undiscussability. There may be a disjunction between IT theory and design with being human. But, when IT is implemented, it is accomplished by the same features that the above authors warn against.[3]

KNOWLEDGE CREATION AND MANAGEMENT

The objective of this stream of research is to understand how organizations create knowledge (Krogh, Ichijo, and Nouaka (2002), Nouaka, Toyana, and Byosiene (2001)). Knowledge is defined as justified belief (with a greater emphasis on 'justified'). Knowledge is created in specific action contexts. Knowledge is created in social interactions between individuals within and across organizations. It is a dynamic human process of tailoring personal belief toward the 'truth'.

The authors cited above propose an interesting multi-layered model of knowledge creation. The model proposes four modes of knowledge conversion; it contains four layers of interacting knowledge.

1. Knowledge creation through processes of socialization, externalization, combination, and internalization (SECI).
2. Knowledge conversion between tacit and explicit knowledge.
3. Ba, the platform for knowledge creation.
4. Knowledge assets, or the inputs, outputs, and moderation of knowledge creation.

The authors then specify the conditions required to convert these processes into creating high-quality knowledge. In terms of a Theory of Action perspective, the specifications are inventions or solutions to the problem of producing high-quality knowledge. For example:

1. Managers discover new strategies and market opportunities by wandering inside the firm.

[3] Fincham (2002) suggests that successful innovation may form a rhetorical pairing with failure in order to produce effective change.

2. Managers facilitate creative and essential dialogue, 'abductive' thinking, and the use of metaphors to foster concept creation.
3. Managers assemble data used to plan strategies and operations.
4. Managers interact with cross-functional groups. They search for and share new values and thoughts, they share and try to understand management's vision and values by communicating with fellow members.
5. Managers foster a spirit of challenge within the organization.

Several questions come to mind.

1. What are the actual actions and how are they sequenced in order to produce the claims embedded in these inventions? For example, what do the managers say or ask while they are walking around? Is it possible for them to ask or to say things that will unwittingly inhibit the likelihood that they will find new strategies? Is it possible that individuals will cover up their actions in order to minimize or even distort what is going on?
2. What do managers ask or say in order to facilitate creative and essential dialogue? Again, what actions inhibit or facilitate the effective implementation of these inventions?
3. What managerial actions facilitate and inhibit cross-functional dialogue? How does communicating with fellow members by sharing and trying to understand top management vision lead to effective action?
4. Which actions foster and which actions inhibit a spirit of challenge?

The advice specifies how to enable the creation of knowledge, but not how to produce the enablers. The advice does not specify how to implement these enablers. The model purports to understand how to create knowledge, but the model does not specify how to create (implement) the knowledge-creation processes defined by the model.

This does not mean that the model is wrong. It means that the model is not complete enough to account for the actions it is intended to produce. If this is the case, then the normative prescriptions embedded in the model are not testable in everyday life because they are not implementable.

The incompleteness of the model is not an unbridgeable gap. In principle, what is necessary is to define the gaps and fill them. What is more serious is that the model is presented as not having the gaps. The authors appear unaware of the gaps and unaware that they are unaware. If this is the case, then it is useful to ask what causes this unawareness that limits the generalizability and validity of the model that purports to specify how to create knowledge.

To illustrate the point, I focus on 'abductive reasoning'. Nonaka and Takeuchi (1995: 30) quote Niskilas, that what is needed is to truly understand how knowledge is created. This is accomplished by grasping the true meaning of being in the world. The true meaning is that the essential mode is to act on the world, not to cognize it. The difficulty is that the authors' descriptions about creating knowledge are at the level of espoused actions. For example, the authors state that the quintessential example of socialization is the traditional apprenticeship. The apprentice learns through observation, imitation, and practice. The observation, imitation, and practice are based upon the novice's interacting with an expert who is relatively flawless in what he or she is producing. Moreover, much of what the novices observe they can skillfully reproduce or know how to learn to reproduce. A relatively seamless transformation is hypothesized between the expert and the novice.

The traditional apprenticeship, as described, requires that the apprentice learn by observing the actions of the master. The authors describe these actions at the espoused level. They do not specify how the master creates the knowledge that the novice will use to become skillful at creating the knowledge required.

The authors give other examples. Informal meetings are key contexts for socialization; participants talk over meals, which leads to them sharing their world-views. These sessions lead to mutual trust. But in their conceptualization of apprenticeship, the authors do not specify what is said or how it is said. To what extent is the dialogue based on Model I or Model II? If it is Model I, how is trust produced?

Similar issues arise with the discussion on the use of metaphors, analogies, and models. The authors claim that the creation and use of proper metaphors can help human beings to reveal imbalances, inconsistencies, and contradictions. There are no specifications of the features of metaphors that make them more or less effective in producing balance. Even if one had such metaphors, there is no specification on the actions required to produce 'balance' effectively.

One of the key concepts introduced by the authors is ba (roughly, meaning the place). Ba is the platform where knowledge is shared, created, and utilized. There are four types of ba: originating ba, dialoguing ba, systematizing ba, and exercising ba.

Originating ba is characterized by face-to-face interactions in order to capture the full range of feelings, emotions, and experiences. Originating ba is the world where an individual sympathizes or empathizes with others, removing the barriers between the self and others. From originating ba emerges care, love, and trust. Dialoguing ba creates involvement and a willingness to transcend one's own limited perspectives.

In order for these inventions to be used to produce actions, it is necessary to specify the action strategies. For example, what action strategies does ba encourage that produce that full range of emotions and generate sympathy? How are caring, love, and trust produced? Are these consistent with Model I or Model II social virtues or with neither?

How are originating and dialoguing bas created that assure Intel, for example, that the defensive routines described by Burgelman will produce open dialogue, caring, and trust? How can we explain why CEOs who are asked in a ba designed to help a fellow COO (see Chapter 5) develop into a more effective leader actually produce all sorts of defensiveness, blame the COO, and produce this by being skillfully unaware of their skilled incompetence?

It may be that the ba that is described in this chapter does not meet the actions the authors have in mind as causing their bas to be more effective. The difficulty is that, since the designs-in-use are in a black box, it is difficult to test this claim.

Ba can be spontaneously created or it can be built consciously. Ba, state the authors, has to be energized in order to work. The causal conditions for creating ba include actions that produce autonomy, creative chaos, redundancy, requisite variety, love, care, trust, and commitment. How are these conditions to be created?

Recall the Intel story. Top management, and especially Grove, encouraged autonomy and creative chaos. Having several groups working on the same problems encouraged redundancy. Yet we saw that often middle managers implemented the autonomy they were encouraged to produce by covering up, and covering up the cover-up.

We saw that Grove encouraged creative chaos. He also unilaterally reined it in lest it get out of (his) control. The middle managers knew this was going to happen. They even invented strategies for detecting when Grove was likely to become defensive. They also covered up knowledge that was important for Intel to decide if and when it should leave the memory business and get into the microprocessor business. Again, they systematically covered up the fact that they were covering up.

SUMMARY

The key feature of the authors' model is action. Cognizing is necessary, but not sufficient, for capturing being-in-the-world. I suggest that the models used are espoused theories of action. They are inventions or solutions for producing high-quality knowledge. They do to specify the actions required to implement these inventions. They are not theories-in-use.

In order to meet their own standards of action, it is necessary for the models to specify how action is produced. For example, what actions produce effective and ineffective socialization, combination, and internalization? What actions produce effective autonomy, creative chaos, love, care, and trust? What actions produce external and internal commitment? What are the consequences of each upon producing high-quality knowledge?

As we saw in Chapter 1, significantly different actions are required to produce openness by using Model I and Model II theories-in-use. One of the difficulties of the authors' normative approach is that it does not distinguish in action terms what is effective from what is ineffective. For example, actions occur when human beings are producing socialization, internalization, commitment, caring, trust and honesty, and openness. The actions required to produce them read more like 'selling' claims. For example, the authors state that, in order to produce love, caring, trust, and commitment, the knowledge-producers need to be highly inspired and committed to their goal. They also need to be selfless and altruistic. They should be positive thinkers and avoid showing negative thoughts and feelings. They should be creative, imaginative, and driven to act. How are these features produced by human beings in ways that are effective? Grove espoused many of these features, and often acted consistently with this espoused beliefs. He also behaved in ways that were counterproductive, and was unaware that this was the case.

Features of Scholarly Inquiry that Inhibit Double-Loop Learning and Implementable Validity

INTRODUCTION

On the one hand, double-loop learning and implementable validity are acknowledged by scholars as relevant in organizational life. On the other hand, the focus is primarily upon diagnosing the existence of double-loop issues and significantly less upon resolving them in such ways that the solutions have implementable validity.

Why is this so? I suggest three causes. First is the social scientist's belief that the ultimate aim of scholarly work is to describe the universe as completely as possible, and to test the validity of the description through empirical methods. Second is that the research methodologies in good currency in the scholarly community espouse unlimited and unbiased exploration, yet their theories-in-use are biased and limit the unfettered exploration of the universe being studied.

These first two causes of the dysfunctional action of scholars around double-loop learning and implementable validity stem from the fact that social scientists act consistently with the best practices associated with rigorous research. The 'errors' that produce the dilemma are designed, and the maintenance and reinforcement of the designs are also designed. The norms in the scholarly community enable and maintain limitations to double-loop learning and implementable validity.

The third cause is that, whereas social scientists espouse Model II and an open dialectic, their personal theory-in-use, like most human beings, is Model I. Therefore, they too are subject to phenomena such as skilled incompetence and unawareness, plus the use of defensive reasoning.

VALID DESCRIPTIONS OF THE UNIVERSE

The most widely accepted reason for conducting scholarly research is to describe as accurately and as completely as possible the universe, selected (constructed) in order to understand and explain it. The descriptions are typically organized into patterns so that they are generalizable. The patterns describe some forms of causal or correlative relationships. The intended objective of research methodologies is to minimize undetected distortion by testing as robustly as possible the claims derivable from the patterns. The requirements for achieving this are the requirements of internal and external validity.

The emphasis upon description of the universe 'as is' has two consequences. First, this very objective has the unintended consequence of limiting the complete description of the universe 'as is', since a complete description of the universe must eventually include research on how the universe reacts when the existence of its core features are threatened.

In order to conduct descriptive research on non-trivial changes of the universe, scholars must invent and introduce these changes. Such changes are rare because they are not part of the existing universe as constructed. In order for scholars to conduct such research, they require a vision of the new universe that could overthrow the present universe. The emphasis upon theory and research that describes the present universe is unlikely to lead to the implementation of these requirements.

The very step of describing a new universe makes it necessary to focus upon a universe that is normative, because the new universe is created to meet governing values that presently do not exist. These new governing values are subjective because they are produced by choices made by practitioners and scholars. The task of research is now transformed from being descriptive of the universe 'as is' to being descriptive about features of a normative universe.

A move toward a new universe also requires that scholars include in their focus research that produces prescriptive propositions. Prescriptive research is necessary to specify how to get from here to there, where the 'there' is a rare universe. Without such specification, implementable validity will be low.

Finally, the requirement of producing normative and prescriptive research makes it necessary for scholars to become interventionist in the service of double-loop changes. For example, the new universe will not be produced until human beings act differently. In order to implement the Model II versions of caring, concern, honesty, courage, and trust (Chapter 1), human being will have to learn new double-loop learning skills, and new organizational contexts will have to be created that enable and reward such skills. This is not an easy task, because skilled incompetence, skilled unawareness, and organizational defensive routines form an ultra-tight and stable relationship that inhibits such changes.

I should like to illustrate these claims by using two examples. The first illustrates a microeconomic perspective, namely, the Behavioral Theory of the Firm. The second illustrates a narrative-interpretive perspective as found in organizational studies.

THE BEHAVIORAL THEORY OF THE FIRM

Cyert and March (1963) specify four relational concepts at the core of their perspective. They are (1) quasi-resolution of conflict, (2) uncertainty avoidance, (3) problemistic search, and (4) limited organizational learning. Twenty-five years later, in an introduction to a collection of his essays, March (1988) identified four 'heresies' in the eyes of many economists and students of traditional decision-making. They are: (1) the importance of allocating attention, (2) the omnipresence of conflict, politics, and coalition groups, (3) the conception that action involves rules that adapt to experience rather than anticipatory choices, and (4) the importance of ambiguity, preferences, technology, and history.

There is fundamental agreement here between the Behavioral Theory of the Firm and Theory of Action. Both perspectives agree that coalition groups, uncertainty avoidance, limited learning, and quasi-resolution of conflict are central features of the organization. Theory of Action includes these phenomena as part of Model I theories-in-use and organizational defensive routines. The concepts of allocating attention, rules that adapt to experience, and the importance of ambiguity, preferences, and history are consistent with the Theory of Action focus on design and action that is related to theories-in-use.

The divergence of views can be illustrated by the position March takes on concepts such as routines, control, loyalty, and trust. March (1981: 221) states that it is the standard operating procedures and routines that are causally responsible for much of the behavior that is observed in organizations. Mundane rules are at the heart of organizational activity. Rules, in turn, are based upon previous experience and history (1981: 224). If change is to occur, it must be clearly linked to mundane rules (1981: 222). What is the meaning of 'linked?' One reading is that all changes, if they are to persist, have to be linked to routines and procedures. I agree. Double-loop changes, for example, will eventually have to be linked to routines and procedures if they are to persist.

There is a second reading of the term 'linked'. This reading could lead researchers to pay little attention to research that is aimed at double-loop changes in the routines. For example, if it works, don't fix it or question it. The routines are taken for granted. One of the most difficult learning problems organizations face is to learn that they are not able to learn, *and* that the cause of this inability is the focus on what is taken for granted, namely, routines.

If one claims that limited learning, quasi-resolution of conflict, and competitive coalition groups are omnipresent and routine, it is not difficult to see why they are likely to be taken for granted and therefore not likely to be altered. The point is not their doubt that relational variables are likely to change. The point is: why is not such a crucial claim subjected to empirical test? It may be, for example, that learning is limited by the finite and probably unalterable information-processing capacities of the human mind. However, learning can also be limited by organizational defensive routines and Model I theories-in-use.

Next, the concept of control. March states that control is a fundamental process in most organizations, and then links control and conflict in the following way. He suggests that control systems drive conflict systems because once measures are developed to evaluate performance and compliance they invite manipulation. Once the rules of evaluation are set, conflict of interest between the rule setters and the rule followers assures that there will be some incentives for the latter to maximize the difference between the rule setters and the rule followers. It assures that there will be some incentives for the latter to maximize the difference between their score and their effort. 'Any system of accounts is a road map to cheating on them' (March 1981: 22).

The reasoning appears to be as follows. Control processes are fundamental to organization and require the evaluation of performance. People cope with such evaluations by manipulation and cheating. They create coalition groups to bring about and to protect these self-protective processes. If this self-interest is not consistent with the organization's, then more manipulation and cheating will occur. This, in turn, results in more control, in a self-reinforcing process.

March uses similar logic in discussing trust and loyalty, which, he asserts, are hard to find. The problems of trust are exacerbated by organizational politics, which is a central feature of most organizations. 'The first principle of politics is that everyone is rational and no one can be trusted.' There may be a few who can be trusted but they are to be characterized as innocent and naive (March 1981: 210).

The consequence is that the organizations are composed of winners and losers. The players will try to look trustworthy, even though they are not, in order to be trusted by those people who might become winners. It is therefore a palpable feature of organizational life 'that organizations may be validly characterized as individuals and groups pursuing their own interests by the manipulation of information' (March 1988: 6).

This line of scholarly reasoning is similar to that often used by practicing executives. They too believe that low trust and high conflict are fundamental features of organizations, and that the solution is to establish goals and objectives, to communicate priorities, and to monitor how well these are being implemented. Managerial controls play a central role in these activities.

It is not surprising that March (1988: 8) concludes that changes in the domains of conflict and trust are not likely to be effective. Cyert and March (1963) advise readers that the way to deal with conflict is by using local rationality, acceptable decision rules, and sequential attention to goals. The advice would be more implementable if it also dealt with the organizational and group defenses that are causally involved.

THE NARRATIVE-INTERPRETIVE APPROACH

I begin the discussion of the narrative-interpretive approach by focusing on what appears to me to be the mainstream thinking of the scholars who use it. I will focus on three recent scholarly books whose authors strive to develop their own comprehensive perspective about the use of the narrative-interpretive approach.

Gabriel (2000: 239), in describing the beginnings of a theory of organizational storytelling, defines stories as

narratives with plots and characters, generating emotions in narrator and audience through poetic elaboration of symbolic material. The material may be a product of fantasy or experience, including the experience of earlier narratives. Story plots entail conflicts, predicaments, trials, coincidences, and crises that call for choices, decisions, actions, and interactions whose actual outcomes are often at odds with the characters' intentions and purpose.

Boje (2001) defines a narrative as one that organizes a story into a plot and coherence. Boje describes six options for analysis: deconstruction, story networks, intertextuality, causality, plot, and theme. As I interpret Boje's illustrations of the options, each can be used to make sense of the events that were the focus of the narrative. All the approaches are therefore retrospective; descriptions of events that have occurred.

Czarniawska (1999) defines the narrative mode of knowing as organizing one's experience around the intentionality of human action. Key features of a narrative include a plot that organizes events into one meaningful whole, a convincing interpretation for negotiating meaning. Perceived coherence of sequentially, rather than truth or falsehood, is the underlying criterion for the meanings inferred. Czarniawska (1999: 22) suggests that researchers can conduct field research by watching how the stories are made, collecting them, interpreting them ('what do they say?'), analyzing them ('how do they say it?'), and deconstructing (unmasking) them. In doing this the researchers create their own story and may set it against or together with other stories.

There appear to be several important features that the authors agree are central to the narrative approach.

1. Narratives tell stories with a plot that is inferred and organized by the researchers (analytical interpretations). The narratives are typically about events that have been observed. The narratives are therefore reflections, interpretations of events. The primary focus is descriptive.

2. Narratives describe events that are often about conflicts, predicaments, trials, decisions, and choices. This means that the actors in the narrative produced the behaviors observed. In order to do so, actors must have activated theories-in-use. From a Theory of Action perspective, they (the stories and narratives in the books) used Model I theory-in-use and existing organizational defensive routines.

3. Analytical interpretations are conducted within a time perspective that may be called 'research time'. The analysts take whatever time that they require to develop the narrative.

In principle, there can be narratives that tell an opposite story. However, these stories are abstract and are crafted in the form of espoused theories. There is no narrative at the theory-in-use level.

Narratives do not seem to focus on stories intended to change the status quo. One reason is that, if their primary mode is to tell stories about everyday events, it is unlikely that they will focus on events that do not occur. For example, as we saw in the early chapters, the researchers have not focused on intervening in order to create domains that presently do not exist at the level of theory-in-use.

A second reason is that researchers using the narrative approach do not intend to tell the actors in their stories where and how they may be effective and ineffective. They do not advise as to what is wrong or right; they tell good stories.

These features are consistent with the normal-science theory and methodology described above. Narrative scholars do not appear to focus on creating interventions that are intended to produce rare events such as those that would be produced by using Model II and by creating organizational behavioral systems that reward and encourage double-loop learning. Not surprisingly, there is little focus on how to get from here to there. Nor is there a focus on how to re-educate actors in the new skills and theories required to move from here to there.

Narrative scholars may respond that in principle there is no reason why they cannot focus on stories about rare events. I would agree, but add that the narrative approach, as described above, is limited in producing double-loop learning, just as is the case with normal science theory and methodology. It is possible, I suggest, to use the narrative mode to produce double-loop learning with implementable validity. In Chapter 6, I present several illustrations. Once these illustrations are presented, I plan to return to the question: how come the narrative approach shares some important features with the normal-science approach?

I should like to illustrate this phase of the argument by presenting a narrative approach used by Martin (1990) to deconstruct the text of a story told on national television by the CEO of a multinational corporation with a fine reputation for dealing with employees. Martin (1990: 339) quotes the CEO:

We have a young woman who is extraordinarily important to the launching of a major new [product]. We will be talking about it next Tuesday in its first worldwide introduction. She has arranged to have her Caesarean yesterday in order to be prepared for the event... We have insisted that she stay at home and this is going to be televised in a closed circuit television, so we're having this done by TV for her, and she is staying home three months, and we are finding ways of filling in to create this void for us because we think it's an important thing for her to do.

Martin's presentation skillfully deconstructs the text. She shows that text could be interpreted, not as a story of corporate caring and respect for women, but as one of skillfully helping women stay in the traditional dependent and submissive relationship to men and corporations. They are manipulated to believe that they are respected and cared for when the opposite is the case. This is reminiscent of Sennett's argument about how the new capitalism used flexibility to manipulate employees into dependent, submissive relationships. The deconstructive analysis carries the same implicit message that employees, in this case women, can be duped and manipulated.

Deconstruction and the Theory of Action are in agreement on one point. Martin's deconstruction begins with the premise that gender conflicts exist. They are subtle, often beneath the surface, and designed to unjustly subordinate women's legitimate interests to men's and to corporations' interests. There is much empirical research to show that the premise is true. A sub-premise is that gender conflict is harder to detect and more difficult to combat and correct. Again, the sub-premise is true.

One difference between deconstruction and the Theory of Action is that the latter identifies gender problems as part of a larger and more comprehensive problem in organizations. The features that Martin describes about gender conflicts are features of organizational defensive routines. The value of locating gender problems as part of organizational defensive routines is that it provides a theory of how gender problems arise and how they may be reduced. The same theory can be used to derive and test hypotheses about other defensive routines, many of which may serve to reinforce gender conflicts and to deny that denial exists. The same theory makes it unnecessary to connect the legitimacy for such inquiry with a feminist position. Martin does so explicitly. This advantage can be used to reduce the degree of self-referential logic that is used in this case.

Theory of Action has several practical advantages. First, the CEO (and others) would be helped to realize that the processes used to reduce gender conflicts can also be used to resolve other conflicts that are denied, but do exist. The feminist concern now becomes translated into a concern about women *and* men. Second, this helps women to show that they can take the lead in exhibiting overall and not simply parochial (for example, feminist) interests, a danger that Martin is aware of.

The third advantage is that there is a focus on changing mind sets and actions throughout the organization. In deconstruction, there is no focus on engaging the CEO on his skilled incompetence and skilled unawareness. One reason may be that scholars of deconstruction do not claim that their approach reveals 'the' truth. There are, they claim, at least as many truths as there are participants—which may legitimize not asking the CEO what he intended. This strategy makes it less likely that the researcher would have to deal with hostility from the CEO if he felt misunderstood and offended.

Why bypass these possibilities? Would they not help to enrich the understanding of the defensive routines and the tenacity with which they are observed? One hypothesis is that the deconstructionists may also exhibit skilled incompetence and skilled unawareness, and would not feel confident of learning from examining this emotional route.

Another possibility is that the community norms around openness to inquiry may be stronger at the espoused level than they are at the level of theory-in-use. The theory itself, again protected by community norms, argues against the necessity for stipulating that there is one truth. If there are as many truths as there are perspectives, then what sense does it make to confront different perspectives?

It makes a lot of sense if you are a manager who feels a deep sense of responsibility for reducing if not eradicating defensive routines. Bypassing them is a recipe for strengthening defensive routines while denying that this can have the same consequences. Thus, scholars and their community appear to exhibit the same defensive routines as the corporations they seek to study. If this is a reasonable inference, how will scholars ever learn? Also, this may explain the basic position that there are no truths, and hence claims will be never ending. If so, does it not also follow that the participants will create endless defensive routines?

How will scholars of the deconstructionist approach ever find out if and when they are wrong? Indeed, what is the meaning of wrong if it is fundamentally assumed that there are infinite inter-pretations that are, in principle, all correct? This may please the scholars but practitioners may see it as a betrayal of responsibility to help human beings who seek a better world.

There is another problem. In deconstruction, as presented, no attention is paid to helping women examine the way they may encourage and strengthen the defensive routines that they claim suppress them. Do women not exhibit skilled incompetence and skilled unawareness? I am reminded of a conversation with Frere, who told me that the biggest problems he faced in creating emancipatory conditions came from the natives he wanted to emancipate.

There remains the responsibility of influencing those with power. Why was no attention given to ensuring that the CEO and the mother engage in dialogue that would help them to see how they create the problems that they condemn and what construct-ive actions to take to correct the errors they wish to correct? The advice that is instead given to the CEO is to make radical changes in human resources policies, such as to 'make sure' that the baby is delivered before the product, and that the mother is encouraged to be with the baby at the workplace for three (or more?) months.

There is no illustration of the likely dialogue between the CEO and the scholars as to how she would deal with his skilled incompetence and skilled unawareness. Nor is there any dialogue on how to deal with his understandable bewilderment about altering human resources policies by 'placing the mother and child' first and organizational performance second. Nor is there any analysis of what the ethical problems may be (for example, women who choose not to have children). Presumably, if women chose to remain at home, they would be permitted to do so. Is it not possible that some would calculate the financial costs and request reimbursement instead?

Note that all of Martin's recommendations are structural and about creating new policies. This is an important first step. In a later chapter, we will show that, when structural arrangements and policies are instituted to reduce defensive routines, when they are championed by the CEOs, and when the implementers do not have the Model II skills to implement them, the structural changes will be very limited. Structure and policies are important enablers. Theories-in-use are the producers of the enablers.

THE NARRATIVE-INTERSPECTIVE APPROACH AND DOUBLE-LOOP LEARNING

Those using the narrative-interpretive approach will have difficulty in producing propositions about double-loop learning that are implementable, for several reasons. First, they rely on narratives that describe, in the form of stories, what the storyteller inferred happened. Even if everyone agrees to the veracity of the account, the description is of what happened, it is of the universe 'as is'. The narratives that are presented in Boje (2000), Czarniawska (1999), and Gabriel (2000) are about events that took place in a Model I world with organizational defensive routines.

Second, the analysis of the narrative—the analytical interpretation—is conducted after the event occurred. We know something about what happened and about the processes that produced the intended consequences. The analytic interpretation occurs in a 'research' time frame; the analyst takes the time needed to make the analysis and is under no pressure to undertake other tasks. But none of these conditions is likely to be available to human beings who are taking actions in everyday life. This raises the question whether the methodologies used to make a 'complete' analytic interpretation can be useful to someone taking action. I am reminded of a model of organizations that purported to be a valid description of the variables and their interrelationships that could explain much of the organizational behavior. Even if we assumed that it was completely valid, it was so complex that it would be unimplementable by human beings in everyday contexts. The scholars who created the model were aware of this problem, but they saw it as the responsibility of the actor, who would, in the authors' view, have to 'degrade' the rigor of their model (Argyris 1980).

Third, the separation of a poetic interpretation from an analytical one may also inhibit the production of implementable knowledge. Effective action requires on-line reflection (Schön 1983). Such reflection requires the actor to pay attention to poetic and analytic interpretations. The separation may also serve to distance the scholars from the subjects: the antithesis of 'closeness' that narrative scholars claim is important between themselves and their 'subjects'. The distancing surfaces by examining the recommendations scholars make as a result of their analytical-interpretive analyses.

For example, Martin (1990) deconstructed a story of a CEO whose behavior illustrated skilled incompetence and skilled unawareness. Her suggested recommendations bypass these issues; she recommends structural changes that bypass helping the CEO explore his skilled incompetence and skilled unawareness. Engaging the CEO in this manner would demand a closer relationship with the CEO than would be required to implement the structural arrangements that she recommends.

The same is true of Van Maanen's (1982) study of policemen. Van Maanen claims that humanistic-interpretive researchers get close to their subjects. He certainly had close relationships with his subjects; witness the rich dialogue that he reports, including candid comments by some policemen about their behavior toward the citizens they arrest. I think it is fair to say that Van Maanen establishes that police expressed a non-trivial amount of mistrust, hostility, and prejudice toward the citizens they serve. He also documents how this hostility can become internalized by individuals (appearing, for example, as constant swearing) and can be the basis for a police culture that protects such individual defenses.

Van Maanen limits his ethnographic research in ways that respect the distancing the police exhibit toward the citizens they serve. If he could help the police explore the causes of this distancing, he could help them get closer to themselves. Indeed, ethnographers themselves might benefit by exploring the meaning of their collusion with subjects' distancing. One might say that some humanistic-interpretive, or naturalistic, researchers get close enough to know when they are getting too close.

Van Maanen, as far as I can tell, did not conduct research to explore the causes and resiliency of these individual and cultural defenses. This could be done, for example, by developing an intervention program intended to expose and reduce the defenses. I believe Van Maanen would not disagree with this possibility but would maintain that intervention to change taken-for-granted behavior is not part of his research practice. The point that I am making is not that he must change, but that he and other ethnographers ought to specify the distancing that they create, just as they specify the distancing they claim the positivists create.

Using narrative methods that distance the scholars from their subjects, and vice versa, leads scholars using the narrative approach to produce advice that is as abstract as that described in previous chapters developed by the more traditional methods. For example, in an innovative approach to the study of leadership, Grint (2000) studied the records of two leaders in the 'same' situation of a mutiny, where one captain was executed and the other captain became a hero. He also analyzed Florence Nightingale's success in the Crimean War, and her failure to build on this success when she returned to London. There are fascinating analyses of Hitler and Reverend Martin Luther King.

The lesson that he draws about leadership is that leaders actively shape and control the interpretation of the environment, the challenges, the goals, the competition, the strategy, and the tactics. They try to persuade others that their interpretation is both correct and not an interpretation but the truth. This is consistent with a Model I theory-in-use.

Grint goes on to conclude that what makes leaders successful is their subordinates, who protect leaders from their errors. The power of the leaders rests on their subordinates. Leadership problems 'stem not from what our leaders do, but from what we the followers let them get away with' (2000: 419). The problem is how to develop subordinates and organizational cultures that prevent leaders from believing that their positions of responsibility are a reason for absolutism.

Grint advises that leaders are responsible to their followers, as 'in front' but not 'on top', as pulling followers after them', not 'pushing them'. Grint has little to say on how to help educate leaders to produce these conditions in everyday life. He may respond, fairly, that this was not the purpose of his book. He also makes the point that analytical interpretations based on historical data provide fascinating advice for enabling the type of leadership that he recommends, but not for producing the enabling advice.

For example, Grint addresses the following recommendations to leaders:

1. Leaders should divest themselves of their own assumptions, and walk in the shoes of others.
2. Leaders should know when to stop, or get stopped before they achieve their desire to be the greatest ever.
3. Leaders should generate an open organization where followers are encouraged to compensate for the leader's errors, and are free to criticize that leader whenever necessary.

4. If leaders break rules and regulations, they should simultaneously develop a relationship with their subordinates where they do not act in the same manner toward them.

How do Model I leaders with skilled incompetence and skilled unawareness become skillful at divesting themselves of their own assumptions? How do they become skilled at stopping trying to achieve their desire to be the greatest? Even more puzzling is how Model I leaders who are 'required' to keep others out of trouble encourage this feature when they are simultaneously being advised to be in charge and to persuade others that their views are correct and that their truth is not subject to question. Does not such advice place the leader 'on top' of the subordinates? Does it not lead to pushing them? Grove comes close to believing and using these types of leadership. We have seen that the results are mixed.

PLURALISM

Coexisting with the requirement that research should be descriptive is the norm that scholars should be free to select whatever theoretical perspective they prefer (Bolman and Deal 1991; Gill and Johnson 1991; McGrath, Martin, and Kukla 1982; Morgan 1983; Schein 1987a; Scott 1981; Van Maanen 1982). Embedded in this norm is a condition that is taken for granted and rarely raised as an explicit issue, namely, that empirical research should adhere to the requirements of internal and external validity. Implementable validity is not included as a coequal requirement. If it were included, the range of acceptable pluralism would be altered.

For example, Morgan and Smircich (1980) describe two research paradigms, 'interpretist' and 'functionalist'. They describe each paradigm's assumptions about ontology, human nature, epistemology, metaphors, and research methods. The interpretist and functionalist paradigms are placed along a continuum ranging from subjectivist (for the former) to objectivist (for the latter).

The result is a thirty-box table describing the different assumptions that accompany the different degrees of subjectivism and objectivism.

A first reaction to the table is that there are indeed paradigms that are primarily subjectivist and others that are primarily objectivist. However, a second reaction is that the table does not accurately characterize the assumptions regarding ontology, human nature, epistemology, metaphors, and research methods embedded in the theory and research described in this book. The problem is not that only some of the categories in the table are relevant; but that almost all the categories are relevant. For example, an intervention starting with the owner-directors of an organization began with the development of a map (Argyris 1993). The map contained descriptions of the patterns of the director group's defensive routines. The map represents reality as a social construct. It is implemented in a realm of symbolic discourse, is a contextual field of information, and is a representation of concrete processes and structures in the sense that these processes and structures exist 'out there'. It coerces different directors to behave in a similar manner.

The assumptions about human nature illustrated in the research also range from the extremes of subjectivism to those of objectivism as presented in the table. For example, the participants were symbol creators, symbol users, and actors using symbols. There were also information processors with limited capacity to deal with environmental complexity. The same individuals were primarily adapters and responders before and after the interventions.

Finally, the research methods used ranged from explorations of pure subjectivity to script and symbolic analysis, contextual analysis, historical analysis of the director group, and the design and execution of many experiments. Moreover, the entire research project occurred over a period of five years before publication, and is still proceeding. History became increasingly important as the interventions accumulated, but so did the testing and experimenting used to assess the extent to which the new pattern contained processes and structures that 'coerced' action in the service of learning and of reducing defensive routines at all levels.

When individuals, groups, intergroups, or organizations are studied under conditions in which interventions are an integral part of the activity *and* the interventions involve double-loop learning, I suggest that both subjectivist and objectivist assumptions will always be relevant. It is only in theoretical applications that they can be treated as antithetical. For example, we had to help the directors become aware of how they constructed reality (subjectivist). We then helped them see how these constructions led to a pattern that was 'out there', because they had placed it out there through actions designed to inhibit. This, in turn, required us to map contexts and study systems and processes. Finally, this led us to help the directors see how they had created a world in which a positivist stance was both necessary and counterproductive.

When we helped them begin a new pattern, we had to help them learn new metaphors and to keep abreast of the metaphors of theater, culture, cybernetics, and organisms. We also helped them design and implement many experiments in order to create over time a new pattern that was 'out there' and that 'coerced' Model II behavior. Moreover, through the analysis of transcripts we could become as quantitative as we wished in order to assess the impact of the new actions and the patterns the directors were building. Both the old and the new realities produced contexts composed of concrete processes and structures. However, the new pattern included processes and structures to monitor and question those processes and structures.

Our empirical observations about organizational politics are consistent with the major published perspectives on this subject. For example, the directors defined organizational politics as influence activities to obtain ends not sanctioned by the organization and as activities to obtain sanctioned ends through non-sanctioned influence means (Mayes and Allen 1983). The directors' behavior was often self-serving (Sander 1990) and in opposition to the formal organization; it was intended to obtain scarce resources and to build power. Conflict and uncertainty were frequently observed and reported. All these features were consistent with the definition of organizational politics by Drory and Romm (1990). The directors did bargain, negotiate, and jockey for position, especially around the allocation of scarce resources. Although they espoused a lack of enduring differences in values, beliefs, and perceptions of reality, their theories-in-use encouraged these differences. This led to the formation of coalitions within the director group and, later, between members of the director group and those of several groups below the directors. These features are consistent with organizational politics as defined by Bolman and Deal (1991), Daft (1983), Eisenhardt and Bourgois (1988), and Kumar and Ghadially (1989).

The strategy of conducting such interventions is not limited to the pluralistic strategy of using several different perspectives relatively independently of each other. For example, Hassard (1991) has described a study in which four different paradigms (functionalist, interpretive, radical structuralist, and radical humanist) were used to study features of an organization. Each study was conducted consistently with each perspective's assumptions regarding ontology, epistemology, human nature, and methodology. Each produced different descriptions of different features of the organization. There was no attempt reported to produce actionable knowledge relevant to changing the status quo. The exercise met the needs of the researchers, who wanted to see what the different perspectives would produce, and the subjects' interests were subordinated to the researchers' interests. The same is true of Allison's (1971) analysis of the Cuban missile crisis.

The researchers also produced, by design, defensive routines in their relationships with the subjects. For example, they withheld their interest in conducting the research with four different paradigms because they feared that they might not gain access if they revealed their intentions fully. In my view, they bypassed embarrassment and threat and covered up the bypass.

Donaldson (1985) suggests that integrative research, which allows paradigms to be used conjointly, is necessary because integration can lead to increasingly comprehensive theories, a consequence favored by science. Those in the pluralistic camp disagree. They claim that such approaches amount, in effect, to a surrender to the dominant paradigms, such as the functionalist-positivistic. Jackson and Carter (1991: 111) defend paradigm incommensurability because doing so expands 'dramatically the scope of organization studies, the interests represented, and those empowered to speak'. I support the expansion. My argument is that, when we are guided by pluralism, it does not go far enough or deep enough. One way to go further and deeper is to focus on producing actionable knowledge, especially of the variety that leads to double-loop learning. Research that produces such knowledge is interventionist. Since paradigm incommensurability inhibits production of actionable knowledge, the plea for incommensurability, which is intended to avoid domination by any one approach or combination of approaches, may have the unintended consequence of becoming a plea for merely a different kind of scientific authoritarianism.

SCHOLAR DEFENSIVE REASONING AND PLURALISM

When scholars choose their research upon personal preferences that do not take into account implementable validity, they often organize themselves into camps used to protect their choices. This leads to arguments and rivalries that are based upon defensive reasoning. For example, humanistic-interpretative researchers assert, I believe correctly, that positivists strive to be objective. In being objective, they tend to ignore meanings held by their human subjects, because a consideration of those meanings would require an intuitive, subjective, and empathic grasp of the subjects' consciousness (Giddens 1976). They also tend to ignore the processes by which their subjects construct their realities (Rosen 1991). This results in positivistic researchers' distancing themselves from their subjects.

Rosen's (1991) assertion that naturalistic researchers deconstruct the barriers between themselves and their subjects therefore requires more specification. The same is true of his assertion that, since naturalistic researchers deconstruct barriers, their instruments are necessarily flexible and less rigid than those of the positivists. Again, much depends on the meaning of rigidity. For example, if rigidity means that the directions for using the instruments are not to be altered, then the cases that we ask our clients to complete are rigid (Argyris 1993). We do not permit deviance. Indeed, any deviance is seen as possible data about either individual or organizational defensive reactions.

I suggest that a bigger problem with questionnaires, a type of instrument that Rosen queries, is not that they are rigid but that the kinds of data they collect make it difficult to infer the subjects' meanings (Argyris 1976). Questionnaires are typically composed of questions that activate espoused theory answers. Recently attempts have been made to correct this problem by Axenn, Fricke, and Thornton (1991) and Rentsch (1990).

Another position often taken by field researchers who focus on naturalistic observations is that such research goes deeper than does research that is designed to be distant in order to be objective. Again, this position seems plausible. However, there are gaps and inconsistencies to be found, which are illustrated by Dyer and Wilkins's critique (1991) of Eisenhardt's (1989) position on how to conduct research.

Dyer and Wilkins favor using stories to generate theory. They believe that single-case stories can deliver deep insights, while those developed from comparative case studies are likely to be 'thin'. The difficulty is that they craft their position so that it is not unconfirmable. For example, what are the properties of a story? What are the properties of 'thin' insights? Dyer and Wilkins (1991: 616) state: 'Although it is difficult to determine how deep a researcher must go to generate good theory, the classic case study researchers certainly went deeper into the dynamics of a single case than Eisenhardt advocates'. But the authors do not define what an appropriate depth is. Until this is done, how can we judge Eisenhardt's position to be wanting?

One could argue that in-depth insights can come from experiences lasting only a few hours. For example, Kurt Lewin and Roger Barker were highly skilled at observing children at play and immediately related what they saw to concepts of field forces, life space, gatekeeper, frustration, and regression. They had the skill to observe action and connect it to theory (Wheelan, Pepitone, and Abt 1990). They could also learn from lengthy experiences, as Lewin learned about democracy and prejudice by being a Jew in Nazi Germany.

Dyer and Wilkins (1991) assert that in multi-case studies the focus is on the construct to the detriment of the context. I am in favor of focusing on the context; but those of us who support contextual research are, I suggest, responsible for defining context in a way that is not self referential, which makes testing features of it difficult. Dyer and Wilkins approvingly cite several classic case studies that tell a story (for example, Whyte 1991). Yet, as Eisenhardt (1989) shows, those studies had features that were consistent with her view of context as much as, if not more than, with Dyer and Wilkins's view.

Rosen (1991) emphasizes that ethnographers typically collect qualitative and not quantitative data. However, in the intervention study described above (Argyris 1993), the qualitative data could easily be translated into quantitative data. One could count, for example, the frequencies with which human beings advocated, evaluated, and attributed in ways that encouraged inquiry and testing. One could count the number of self-sealing non-learning episodes, such as the self-fueling processes described by Hackman (1989) and his associates. In a later chapter I hope to show that the standards of explanation and internal validity can be met with these simple quantitative procedures because our theory permits robust predictions, because tests can be conducted in changing the status quo, *and* because changing the status quo is such a rare event that, if it is done, one does not need sophisticated quantitative procedures to document it. For example, the dialogues between the CEO and the directors and the evaluation of the

CEO's performance by the directors (Argyris 1993) were rare events. Three years before they occurred, the participants unhesitatingly predicted that such activities were not likely to occur; and, as one director said, ' "not likely to occur" means "until hell freezes over" '.

Finally, Rosen (1991) also suggests that ethnographers do not allow any theoretical preoccupations to decide whether some facts are more important than others. I agree that competent ethnographers focus on relatively directly observable data; for example, we used observations and tape recordings. Both, but especially the latter, could be used by any researchers with significantly different theories to test our generalizations or to develop tests of their own.

It is difficult to agree, however, that ethnographers do not allow any theoretical preconceptions to decide whether some facts are more important than others. As I see it, by eschewing interventions to change the constructed world they describe, they ignore, or do not permit to surface, the data that would arise if anyone tried to change that world. They may not let their preconceptions decide which facts are and are not important. But they allow their preconceptions to create conditions under which crucial facts will never be revealed.

Rosen (1991: 21) quotes Kunda as saying that 'ethnography is the only human activity in the social sciences . . . [that] is not divorced from the modes of experience that I consider human'. I do not doubt that Kunda considers ethnography to be connected to what it means to be human, but the validity of the assertion is, in my judgement, doubtful. Kunda's study, which in my opinion is an excellent example of ethnography, misses the core of what it means to be human, according to *his* standards. Being human means to act, to construct a world, and to engage the world in ways that engage the actors. Kunda observed human beings 'being human', but Kunda never became human in the sense of taking action to help his subjects in the struggle to be human. It was possible for Kunda to become as human as his subjects by developing interventions. Interventions are human experiments that have the purpose of constructing different virtual worlds.

THE THEORY-IN-USE OF RESEARCH METHODOLOGY

I now turn from the unintended consequences of focusing primarily upon describing the universe 'as is' to a discussion of the research methodologies used by scholars conducting normal-science research.

Research is implemented in a relationship between researchers and their subjects. Researchers have concluded that in order to implement research that maximizes internal and external validity, it is necessary to create human relationships with subjects that have the following features:

- the researchers are in control of the final definition of how the research is framed;
- the researchers also keep secret from subjects any knowledge that might distort their responses;
- the researchers design their research implementation in ways to minimize negative feelings by the subjects; and
- the researchers control the time perspective.

All this is consistent with Model I governing variables.

There are three consequences of using this Model I theory-in-use. The first consequence is tacit. Can it be made explicit by focusing on how a user could implement the knowledge in the generalizations? For example (Argyris 1980):

1. From some of the most sophisticated research on mass communications the following advice could be derived. If you are trying to persuade an audience to choose an option or stance, and if you consider the audience to be composed of human beings who are not so bright, describe only one option. If the audience is considered 'bright', describe several options. Imagine what would happen if those communicating to a 'dumb' audience state that they are providing them with one option because science recommended that they deal with not-so-bright audiences in this way.

2. Scholars advised activists who were against the Vietnam War how to lie and spin to get their foot in the door, in order to convince the listener of the injustice of the War and to cover up that this was what they were doing.

3. Scholars quoting reactance theory advised individuals on how to manipulate people into buying window shades that were often unneeded and in many cases would not fit the windows for which they were being bought. Most of the buyers were poor.

4. Scholars using reinforcement learning theory advised executives how to reward their subordinates in ways that required the use of reinforcement schedules that were covered up. These schedules would work if the subordinates behaved as dutifully as did the animals in the experiments where the results were originally produced.

The second consequence of Model I used in conducting research is that, in order to implement the generalizations, any scholar would have to use Model I strategies. For example, Barker, Lewin, and Dembo (1941), in a careful, systematic, experimental study, reported that frustration led to regression and also that mild frustration led to creativity.

Let us picture a leader who wishes to use this knowledge to enhance her group's creativity. How would she go about implementing their finding? Would the leader tell her group members that she intends to frustrate them mildly in order to enhance their creativity? How would she assess when mild frustration was produced and when it was exceeded? How would she stop it when the frustration became too high? Solid answers to these questions require the scholars to spell out in precise terms the instruments to be completed by research assistants who were observing behind one-way mirrors. Moreover, it took them days to analyze the data.

Think also of the group members. How would they react to learning about her strategy? How would they react to periodic attempts to measure their frustrations? What kinds of measures would they be? If they were intrusive, would that not be a major act of manipulation and cover-up?

The third consequence in the embedded and tacit use of Model I raises a question about the claim made by descriptive researchers that they are neutral. The research is not neutral, because (1) its generalizations are biased toward Model I, (2) the methods used to implement the generalizations are consistent with Model I, and (3) the generalizations are sufficiently abstract that they do not differentiate between Model I and other alternatives.

The last consequence becomes apparent when researchers describe contexts that are different from Model I. For example, an organic organization (Burns and Stalker 1961) is associated with Model II. But, if my above analysis is correct, how could that happen? I claim that the generalizations will be consistent with Model I. The answer is that the organic organization espouses Model II, but the theory-in-use is Model I. The authors do not make this distinction; the concept is defined and illustrated in such abstract terms that its Model I features are not made explicit.

For example, the work by Burns and Stalker (1961) has been used to assert that in the social universe there is a 'fit' or 'balance' among individual needs, organizational requirements, and environmental demands. Scholars tend to equate Model II with organic systems and Model I with mechanistic systems. Thus, organic systems are described as being more open to learning, more flexible, and less concerned about rigid structures than mechanistic systems. Moreover, organic systems are thought to be more functional in turbulent environments, and mechanistic systems more functional in stable environments. This view of the world ignores the possibility that mechanistic organizations that cannot double-loop learn may be unable not only to detect and correct error, but also to detect their failures to detect and correct error. The result may be that actions can be taken within the organization that are wrong and that sow the seeds for creating a turbulent environment. Hence, the 'fit' of mechanistic systems to stable environments could lead to difficulties for the system (Argyris 1972).

If we examine the relatively directly observable data in the Burns and Stalker (1961) study, a case could be made that organic systems are oscillating Model I systems. For example, one finds claims like the following:

1. Weekly meetings between management and employees were largely 'briefing sessions' (1961: 87) because anything abnormal had been dealt with by other people and had been translated into the normal and routine.
2. Foremen were expected to speak up, but 'it is also expected that persons of lower rank in the hierarchy of management will exercise their right to speak in a more discreet fashion than their seniors' (1961: 88).
3. In an organization, 'the head of the concern stands for the concern and its relative success—he symbolizes or personifies it. The system and structure of management are both determined largely by him. Above all, he is the ultimate authority for appointments and promotion' (1961: 21).
4. An organization can be made more organic with centrally controlled flexibility. For example, 'tight central control with the object of enabling production, resources, managerial and design efforts... to be changed quickly [by the top] as the situation demanded' (1961: 225).
5. Conditions that tend to make it difficult to raise questions and to voice criticisms (for example, differences in status and power were muted by games, such as everyone calling each other 'chief' and the director calling everyone 'governor' (1961: 253).

For example, the following excerpt from Burns and Stalker (1961: 253) is from an interview in an organic system:

x:... everybody is approachable by everybody else. It seems to me that it is almost a tradition here that that is so.
INT: And it is not particularly cultivated?... Or is it cultivated?
x: It is natural. I suppose, to some extent. People with long service in the organization just naturally do it, you see, and people coming in from outside, I suppose, just follow on. They can't do anything else, you see, because...

INT: You can't act stuffy among a crowd like that?

x: No. No. You see, if the paint sprayer comes up with something and says, 'Well, here you are, chief', there's nothing much you can do about it, even if you want to. Which he does, you see; everybody calls everybody else 'chief' here, whoever they are. Except Mr. A. (a director)—he'll call everybody 'governor'.

INT: Well, that's a nice way of smoothing over status differences. If everybody is 'chief', then there are no differences between people to bother about.

x: Yes, that's right. Nobody can complain.

Apparently the device of calling everyone 'chief' is seen as a genuine leveler and of 'inestimable value'. Whenever there is potential difficulty because of status differences, 'the ability to pitch what one says into a half-jocular style that explicitly rejects the pressure or sanction one could bring to bear is of enormous value. The social technique of doing this—the accepted formula used in this firm—was trivial. The fact that it could be successfully employed was all important' (Burns and Stalker 1961: 253).

Embedded in these assertions about organic systems are Model I top-down theories-in-use and organizational defensive routines. For example, in the above list of claims, (1) top management decided what was to be translated into the routine; in (3) it is the top that personified success and defined the nature of the system and structure of management; and in (4) the organic flexibility was centrally controlled and manipulated. Examples (2) and (5) describe the games that people played in order to speak out yet maintain the top-down authority structure.

The point is that the reality that people experience on different levels not only may vary but also may be inherently contradictory. For example, according to Burns and Stalker (1961), the mechanistic and organic structures have the properties set out in Box 5.1.

If people are programmed with a Model I theory-in-use, they will behave in either type of organization according to their theory-in-use. In the case of the organic organization, there will be a discrepancy between the structure and the behavior. For example, although authority is vested in the person who can deal with the

Box 5.1. Mechanistic and organic structures compared

Mechanistic structure	Organic structure
Great division of labor and specialization of tasks.	The person with the specialist knowledge goes wherever needed.
Clear hierarchy of authority.	Authority is vested in the person who can deal with the problem.
Precise definition of job, duties, rules, etc.	Continual redefinition of individuals' jobs as the situation requires.
Centralization of information and decision-making.	Information and knowledge may be located anywhere in the organizational network.
Preponderance of vertical communication.	Preponderance of horizontal communication.

problem (organic), that person will behave in ways that make clear who has the power (mechanistic). Although there may be redefinition of jobs (organic), as the foregoing material illustrates, there is a precise and unchanging definition of the rules of how to show deference (mechanistic). Although the communication may be horizontal (organic), the meanings produced within these communications will tend to be consonant with the vertical (mechanistic).

Another problem is the one illustrated by the work of Morse and Lorsch (1970), who found that the managers in a mechanistic organization felt very satisfied and committed and that they expressed a sense of competence and high motivation to perform work that was routine, highly predetermined, and under leaders who made the decisions. But why did the managers feel a sense of satisfaction, commitment, and competence under these conditions? Morse and Lorsch say it was because they accepted orders, performed their jobs well, and therefore felt a sense of success and effectiveness. An alternative explanation may be that they, the managers, were obeying the dictates of a hierarchy.

Unfortunately, we cannot decide between the two explanations because the study used projective techniques that produce espoused theories. For example, Morse and Lorsch (1970) report that the employees were satisfied, committed, and productive (in a Model I, mechanistically organized system) because they experienced a sense of competence. Competence, they argue, is a basic need; because a basic need is being fulfilled, morale is positive.

The logic makes sense if the criterion for competence in the heads of the employees is not affected by the environment. But that criterion can be significantly influenced by the environment in which they work. If we examine the criteria of competence that Robert White (1959) uses and the one used by the managers, we find some important differences (see Box 5.2).

Box 5.2. White's and managers' criteria of competence

White's criteria	Managers' criteria
Emphasizing novelty.	Emphasizing sameness and routine.
Having few predetermined rules. Producing further difference in sameness.	Having many predetermined rules. Staying within the differences permitted.
The subsiding of motivation when a situation has been explored and presents no new possibilities.	The continuing of motivation even when a situation presents no new possibilities.
Experimentation.	Minimal experimentation.
Striving toward autonomy.	Striving toward submissiveness.
Tending to vary behavior.	Tending to repeat behavior.

These are different states of affairs. Indeed, as Morse and Lorsch suggest, the managers' morale would probably plummet if they were thrust into jobs that were characterized by White's criteria.

Bazerman, Curhan, and Moore (2000: 200), as a result of an extensive review of the literature on negotiation, recommend that more attention be paid to how to make the practice more effective. Their arguments begin with a description of fundamental skills exhibited by negotiators. These include the following:

- to be inappropriately affected by the positive or negative frame in which risks are viewed;
- to anchor their number estimates in negotiations on irrelevant information;
- to rely too heavily on readily available information;
- to be over-confident about the likelihood of attaining outcomes that favor themselves;
- to assume that negotiation tasks are necessarily fixed-sum and thereby miss opportunities for mutual beneficial trade-offs between parties;
- to escalate commitment to a previously selected course of action when it is no longer the best alternative;
- to overlook the valuable information that can be obtained by considering opponents' cognitive perspective; and
- to reactively devalue any concession that is made by the opponent.

It is unlikely that negotiation practice will be effective if those involved use irrelevant information, are over-confident, assume fixed-sum results and thus miss opportunities for mutually beneficial negotiation, overlook valuable information, and devalue concessions made by opponents. Therefore, these are errors or mismatches.

How do the authors explain these systematic errors? They suggest that individuals construe the world, and then behave in ways that are self-serving. This predisposition is called 'egocentrism' by the authors. Egocentric actions have dysfunctional consequences such as the fundamental biases described above. Another set of causes is what the authors call 'motivated illusions', which include unrealistically positive views of the self, unrealistic optimism, the illusion of control, and self-serving attributions. Data are presented to illustrate these phenomena. Again, the causal mechanisms by which human beings produce these illusions appear to be lacking.

Behavioral research provides important insights into action that inhibits the effectiveness of negotiation. It does not, I suggest, explain why so many negotiators have a theory-in-use that leads them to produce the fundamental biases and motivational illusions. How do negotiators become skilled at producing these behaviors? How come they construe the world in ways where they either do not recognize the errors that they are making or, if they do, place the blame on others? If they do not recognize the errors, why is this the case? If they do recognize the errors but blame others, then what leads them to believe that making attributional errors (blaming others) is the effective action to take?

Let us reflect on the nature of these explanations. The claim that individuals construct their world and then behave in ways that are self-serving is consistent with the assumption that the purpose of research is to describe the universe and then to infer explanations. But the same commitment, as we have seen, is unlikely to help individuals create a different world, where their behavior will be self-serving but to a different set of consequences. Imagine a group of negotiators who become skilled at Model II and, over time, are also able to create a community of practice that minimizes organizational defensive routines. Negotiators who are skillful at using Model II will be vigilant at detecting and correcting the biases identified by the authors. For example, they will pay attention to the degree to which their actions may be inappropriately affected by their use of irrelevant information, by relying upon readily available information, and by overlooking valuable information. These negotiators will be aware that Model I governing variables inhibit double-loop learning because the focus is upon winning, unilateral control, and suppressing negative feelings.

Bazerman, Curhan, and Moore (2001) make the following recommendations:

1. Make managers aware of the potential adverse impact of using heuristics and biases so that they can decide when and where to use them.
2. Give feedback about overconfidence that will reduce moderately that bias.
3. Reduce overconfidence by asking people to explain why their decision-making processes might be wrong.
4. Identify the psychological factors that feed escalation behavior (the key to eliminating non-rational escalation).
5. Teach individuals to search vigilantly for disconfirming data. Establish sound monitoring systems.
6. Get individuals to assess new decisions from a neutral reference point.

The first difficulty of this advice is that it is not connected to the theories- in-use of the people being advised. If their theory-in-use is Model I, then making them aware of their biases or of the overconfidence that they produce is necessary but not sufficient. Negotiators programmed with Model I do not have the skill that the advice requires if they are to reduce the adverse effects of the Model I-induced biases.

In one example, as we shall see in Chapter 7, a group of CEOs role-play helping a senior executive become a more effective leader. The executive has become aware of the counterproductive features of his biases and of his blindness to his counterproductive impact. Yet he is unable to act more effectively. His theory-in-use is Model I. He is skillfully unaware of his skillful incompetence and lacks the Model II skills to produce new actions.

To compound the problem, the CEOs who attempted to advise him also used Model I. The person being advised found their advice abstract and not helpful. The advisers, in turn, reacted by attributing that he was closed to learning. As we shall see, they created a set of self-reinforcing, self-sealing actions that inhibited double-loop learning. How do we move from awareness to action when the individuals do not have the skills to implement the advice and work in a defensive world that inhibits double-loop learning? This question, to date, does not appear to concern the authors of the review paper, nor the many authors cited in the extensive review of others' empirical work.

EXPLAINING SCHOLARS' DEFENSIVENESS BY USING DEFENSIVE REASONING

In a critique (Argyris 2004a) of the development of double-loop learning research, Miner and Meziac's (1996) argument does include awareness that learning is about detecting *and* correcting error. New understanding and insights are necessary but not sufficient. For example, detecting and correcting competency, traps of competency, and destroying actions are, in their view, candidates for research on double-loop learning. The difficulties are illustrated by the studies they cite. The research results are crafted at the espoused level; the authors do not provide actionable knowledge required to correct these problems.

The authors acknowledge that scholars may exhibit defensiveness but this may be due to the infancy of the research. They advise that one of the most valuable ways to reduce scholars' defensiveness is to conduct research that provides compelling evidence of alternative viewpoints. But the literature cited in this book does not support their claim; Burgelman, for example, states that he does not focus on defensive routines because they are not alterable. March's claim that this stance is also true for such concepts as trust raises doubts about the authors' optimism on how to get scholars to focus on their defensiveness. Burgelman states that his stance could create a self-fulfilling prophecy. It is doubtful that compelling evidence could have the optimistic consequences claimed by the authors.

Miner and Meziac (1996) differentiate between routine 'incremental learning' and 'radical learning'. Incremental learning is akin to single-loop learning. One difficulty with this position may be illustrated by recalling the Intel case, in which a movement from memory products to microprocessors was evidence of radical learning. The dominant pattern of learning was single-loop because it was based on scientific and engineering research methods that the executives were skillful at using. Double-loop learning was not involved.

The same was true for the learning actions taken to dislodge the top management from its commitment to memory products. For example, many presentations were made to convince the top that microprocessors could be produced and could achieve the high profit margins required by company policy. These features of the discussion were informed by rigorous productive reasoning. No new governing values were involved.

Burgelman (2002a) also describes middle managers' strategies of how to act so as not to make the top too defensive. They withheld information, such as when many at the top were committed to memory products out of nostalgia. They managed the information given to the top about the defensive routines and covered-up that they were doing so. These are all Model I behavioral strategies. No new governing variables were involved.

The Van de Ven and Polley (1992) study described in Chapter 3 presented rich descriptions of the competitive, defensive group dynamics and organizational politics that were instrumental in facilitating the failure to introduce the new product. Consistent with Model I, these actions were covered up and the cover-up was covered up.

Further evidence of the unlikely consequence of moving some scholars to study double-loop issues and to produce propositions with implementable validity comes from the kind of research needed to close the gap. For example, they call for more descriptive research, the very research that historically has not led to double-loop learning and change. Some scholars claim that the results of sound descriptive research accumulate and eventually make knowledge more actionable. That claim may be true for single-loop learning, but the material in this book and in Argyris (1980: 1993) provide disconfirming evidence as far as double-loop learning is concerned.

Lipshitz (2000) suggests that there is wide recognition among scholars about the importance of double-loop learning. He also states that there is a gap between the recognition of the concept and the amount of research conducted by scholars. He suggests that one reason for the gap is that skill in double-loop learning is not easy to develop. Edmondson (1996) and Senge (1990) support this view based on their personal experience. Lipshitz (2002) and Friedman (2002), who have produced important empirical intervention research on double-loop learning, suggest that the issue of difficulty is relevant.

Possible solutions to these problems can be found in the history of educating scholars. For example, similar arguments were made years ago about the difficulties in learning quantitative skills. What would happen if researchers were offered the opportunity to learn these skills at the same level of course offerings as those available for learning quantitative skills? Some of my graduate students who developed a mastery in intervention activities for double-loop learning did so by meeting periodically to reflect on their practice. Do not graduate students develop their mastery in quantitative methods by teaching sections in that field?

Part of the problem may be that there are few faculty members in research-oriented departments who claim to be competent in teaching these skills. Hence, there are very few courses offered for those interested in conducting such research. A second-order consequence is that, since there are few courses, young scholars who seek to develop their own skills by teaching small seminars find few teaching opportunities to do so.

The lack of opportunity in universities for developing skills in producing actionable knowledge is documented in a recent NIMH (2001) study, *Translating Behavioral Science into Action*. This leads to (1) a growing fragmentation and specialization, and unfamiliarity with other disciplines, (2) a lack of research cooperation between basic and action research, (3) a split between the education and training they receive, and (4) an unawareness of the value of action research for understanding important problems. The report also concludes that investigators, especially new ones, report significant barriers and disincentives to developing careers where action and implementable validity are central. Included in these disincentives are their evaluation about their own competencies to evaluate such research and the doubts about such research on the part of peer review committees.

One way to begin to extricate ourselves from this dilemma may be to create a mini-version of the educational programs supported by the Ford Foundation to educate and re-educate faculty in business schools in such disciplines or economics, psychology, and sociology as well as quantitative methods. Another part of the problem is that research opportunities are limited because organizations hesitate to invite researchers to conduct double-loop learning opportunities if they lacked the skills to do so.

CONCLUSIONS

There is interest in double-loop learning, but at the espoused level. None of the authors cited deal with these issues at the theory-in-use level. The research on learning is in its infancy. It is unlikely that research designed and implemented by theories that favor the status quo and executed by methods based on Model I theories will move toward the double-loop learning that would be required to provide evidence that the claim that defensive routines exist is flawed. For example, Burgelman and March acknowledge that they exist but claim they are not correctable. They also, by design, do not seek to test these claims. The belief that the best way to get scholars to examine their defensive routines is to have them do it privately is flawed. Recall that Burgelman states, in effect, that he is not acting defensively. Yet he also admits his actions could create a self-fulfilling prophecy.

6

Interventions that Facilitate Double-Loop Learning

In this chapter I describe several intervention strategies that can be used to help individuals diagnose the degree to which they adhere to a Model I theory-in-use, and thus produce and maintain organizational defensive routines. The focus is on helping individuals reflect upon their skilled incompetence and skilled unawareness, and their counterproductive consequences.[1]

The first illustration describes a case method called the left-hand/right-hand case method, which we have found to be effective in producing the learning described above. The context is a top management group in a large organization, often described in the literature as an organic group.

The second illustration uses the same case method to produce the same learning results in large group settings composed of up to 150 participants who are strangers to each other.

The third illustration uses a case that describes how Andy, who was hired as a Chief Operating Officer with a promise to become the next CEO, was fired after six months. It will be shown how this case can be used to test features of Model I following the rules of conducting a quasi-experiment.

---

[1] For other interesting interventions that focus on double-loop learning and implementable validity, see Lipshitz (2002), Lipshitz and Popper (2002), Friedman, Lipshitz, and Overmeer (2001), and Robinson (1993).

The fourth illustration describes a learning context where the participants can focus on the degree to which they use defensive reasoning to produce consequences that they do not intend, and indeed that they espouse as being counterproductive.

The first three illustrations can be used as the basis for a quasi-experimental test of features of the Theory of Action approach. For example, the causal claim is made that the Model I theory-in-use is a primary cause of defensive reasoning and its counterproductive consequences for learning. The organizational defensive routines, such as the generic anti-double-loop learning syndrome, feed back to reinforce the Model I theory-in-use. But they are secondary causes. This means that, if we place human beings in situations where the system processes support double-loop learning, and if the human beings use Model I theory-in-use, they will create consequences that are counter to double-loop learning. The seminars described in the first three examples can be used to test these claims. The Andy case is used to illustrate how it can be used to approximate the requirements of a field quasi-experiment.

The test embedded in the three examples is as follows. If individuals are placed in settings that:

(1) are non-hierarchical or pyramidal,
(2) are free from everyday pressures related to achieving organizational objectives,
(3) do not reward or punish people for learning,
(4) do not harm their reputation or their organization,

and if

(5) they are free to leave the setting, and
(6) they choose to attend these settings because they wish to learn how to strengthen their effectiveness in managing themselves and others, as well as designing and implementing effective organizations,

then these individuals will create actions that are consistent with Model I and 'classroom' defenses that are themselves consistent with organizational defensive routines, even though such actions are seen by them and the faculty as counterproductive. Indeed, in the case of these seminars, the individuals are attending to learn how to present the counterproductive consequences.

THE LEFT-HAND/RIGHT-HAND CASE METHOD

The case method illustrated in this section begins with a story that each participant writes beforehand. The key features of this case method in particular are as follows:

1. It produces relatively directly observable data such as conversation. Such data are the actual productions of action, and therefore can become the basis for inferring theories-in-use.
2. It produces data in ways that make clear the actors' responsibility for the meanings produced. When used properly, the respondents cannot make the research instrument causally responsible for the data that they produced (for example, 'I didn't really mean that' or 'I didn't understand the meaning of that term').
3. It produces data about the respondents' causal theories, especially those that are tacit because they are taken for granted.
4. It provides opportunities for the respondents to change their responses without impairing the validity of the inferences being made. Indeed, the actions around 'changing their minds' should also provide data about their causal reasoning processes. It provides opportunities to change their actions as well as the actions of groups, intergroups, and organizations over which they have some influence. It provides such knowledge in ways that are economical and do not harm the respondents or the context in which they are working.

The directions to write a case are given to each individual. The directions are as follows:

1. In one paragraph, describe a key organizational problem as you see it.

2. Assume you could talk to whomever you wish in order to begin to solve the problem. Describe, in a paragraph or so, the strategy that you would use in this meeting.
3. Next, divide your page into two columns. On the right-hand side write how you would begin the meeting—what you did or would actually say. Then write what you believe the other(s) did or would say. Then write your response to their response. Continue writing this scenario for two or so double-spaced typewritten pages.
4. In the left-hand column, write any idea or feeling that you would have that you would not communicate for whatever reason.

In short, the case includes:

- a statement of the problem;
- the intended strategy to begin to solve the problem;
- the actual conversation that did or would occur as envisioned by the writer; and
- the information that the writer did or would not communicate for whatever reason.

Box 6.1 presents a collage of comments taken from cases written by executives who were focusing on getting a greater emphasis on customer service.

Reflection on the Cases

In analyzing their left-hand columns, the executives found that each side blamed the other side for the difficulties, and they used the same reasons. For example, each side thought about the other side:

- 'You do not really understand the issues.'
- 'If you insist on your position, you will harm the morale that I have built.'
- 'Don't hand me that line. You know what I am talking about.'
- 'Why don't you take off your blinders and wear a company hat?'

Box 6.1. A collage from several cases

Thoughts and feelings not communicated	Actual conversation
He's not going to like this topic, but we had to discuss it. I doubt that he will take a company perspective, but I should be positive.	I: Hi, Bill. I appreciate the opportunity to talk with you about this problem of customer service versus product. I am sure that both of use what to resolve it in the best interests of company. BILL: I'm always glad to talk about it, as you well know.
I better go slow. Let me ease in.	I: There are an increasing number of situations where our clients are asking for customer service and rejecting the off-the-shelf products. My fear is that your salespeople will play an increasingly peripheral role in the future. BILL: I don't understand. Tell me more.
Like hell you don't understand. I wish there was a way I could be more gentle.	I: Bill, I am sure you are aware of the changes [and explains]. BILL: No, I do not see it that way. It's my salespeople that are the key to the future.
There he goes, thinking as a salesman and not as a corporate officer.	I: Well, let's explore that a bit...

- 'It upsets me when I think of how they think.'
- 'I'm really trying hard, but I'm beginning to feel this is hopeless.'

Redesigning their Actions

The next step was to begin to redesign their actions. Each executive selected an episode that he wished to redesign so that it would not have negative consequences. As an aid in their redesign, the executives were given some handouts that described the Model II set of behaviors. The first thing they realized was that they would have to slow things down. They could not produce a new conversation in milliseconds, as they were accustomed to do. This troubled them somewhat, because they were impatient to learn. They had to keep reminding themselves that learning new skills did require them to slow down and to practice a lot.

Practice is important. Most people require as much practice to learn Model II as is required to play a not so decent game of tennis. However, the practice does not need to occur all at once; it can occur in actual business meetings where people set aside some time to make it possible to reflect on their actions and correct them. An outside facilitator can help them examine and redesign their actions, just as a tennis coach might do. But, as in the case of a good tennis coach, the facilitator should eventually be unnecessary. The facilitator might be brought in for periodic 'boosters' or to help when the problem is of a degree of difficulty and intensity not experienced before.

CONDUCTING DIAGNOSES IN LARGE GROUPS

In this section I show how the left-hand/right-hand case methodology can be used in large groups in order to educate participants about their respective theories-in-use. If the audience is from many different organizations, it will also generate data about the ubiquitous existence and power of organizational defensive routines. If the participants come from the same organization, the data they generate can be used to develop solutions to defensive routines.

Each participant is asked to submit a left-hand/right-hand case beforehand to the Faculty Member (FM) or leader. The submission of a case is used as a ticket for admission. The reason for this is that the dynamics of a classroom can inhibit learning if the individuals do not have a personal stake in the diagnosis. When they are asked to compare the diagnosis made by the leader with their own case, it is important that participants have written a case; otherwise, they could easily distance themselves from becoming involved. The distancing often influences their responses; moreover, due to skilled unawareness, the class members will not be aware of the distancing.

A Collage of the Left-Hand Columns

The first step is to diagnose the comments in the left-hand column. This column represents any thoughts and feelings that the writers had that they decided to keep secret or censor. They were told beforehand that they would not be required to disclose their reasons.

The Faculty Member reads every case beforehand in order to develop a collage of comments that do not identify the writers. The collage represents as wide a range of comments as possible. Although most comments are consistent with Model I, the FM should especially seek comments that are consistent with Model II. They should be included in the collage without being identified as such. It is important to see whether the participants can tell the difference.

There are a few comments that are not assignable to either Model I or Model II. For example, simple questions do not provide enough data to score them as consistent with Model I or Model II. These questions do provide cues—for example, 'what the hell are you driving at?' But for the most part the questions are typically like 'how do you feel about your performance?' 'Are you concerned?' These can be scored as inquiry. But more information is needed to assign them to Model I or Model II (or some other) status. Often such comments signify an intention to ease in. The individuals ask questions in such a way that they cannot be held responsible for any defensiveness on the part of the respondent. Easing-in questions are consistent with Model I because the purpose of easing in is hidden and not discussable.

In Box 6.2, a collage is developed from two classes of second-year business students. The total number in each class was approximately 150. These comments illustrate the patterns that we find in a wide variety of settings whenever we use this case method. The left-hand column contains thoughts and feelings that are critical for learning to occur. Yet they are systematically covered up. The cover-up is also covered up. In all cases the action strategies are consistent with Model I. For example, as numbered in Box 6.2, we find the following illustrations:

1. Advocates a strategy where he or she is in unilateral control and the other's criticisms are evaluated as wrong.
2. Makes attributions that others are patronizing. There is no inquiry into or test of the attribution. Generates unilateral strategies and acts as if he is not doing so.
3. Adopts a process of cover-up and acts as if he/she is not doing so.
4. Suppresses feelings and advocates a process of being in unilateral control.
5. Makes attributions about others and does not test them. Plans a unilateral act of 'kill'.
6. Evaluates other's behavior as wrong, but does not test the validity of the evaluation.
7. Makes a series of attributions about the other but does not test them. Plans a unilateral effort to make the other a team player by 'using' his ego.
8. Manipulates and covers up. Does not test the validity of the evaluations and attributions that were made to decide to manipulate and cover up.
9. Covers up important information. Covers up the cover-up. Reassures self that change can be made later.

Box 6.2. Collage of columns entitled: what I thought and felt, and didn't say

1. Time to be tactful, yet direct. I must accept his criticism, but make it clear that he does not have the right interpretation.
2. Great. Try patronizing me. That won't get you far... I'm not going to back down... He cares about trust... Talk trust.
3. I want to start this process by agreeing with him. It will be easier to get him to see my viewpoint later.
4. I want to cover my ass in the event that she has issues with my performance at year-end.
5. Be careful. I am getting upset. Stay calm... I should go ahead and say everything I planned. He should not be leading the discussion.
6. I am losing her, so I have to go in for the kill.
7. Bullshit.
8. Defensive individual. May not be as capable as he thinks, or may think his background can allow him to do anything with little effort... Use his ego to make him a team player.
9. Say something nice first. Ease the flow of any negative feedback. Let him know that we are both learning... Be nice... Make excuses.
10. Don't show your entire hand. This is going to be a delicate balance. Once in the team, there will be ample opportunity to make changes.

The comments provide insight into the private thoughts of the individuals. Recall that these thoughts were kept private because the individuals believed that that was necessary if they were to be in control and to achieve their objectives. During the discussions they often said that their reasons for keeping their thoughts and feelings private was that revealing them would likely make the other defensive. This prediction is likely to be true because, if they made public their Model I thoughts, the others would have legitimate reasons for becoming defensive.

What is less often discussed is that their Model I cover-up strategies, if made public, would undermine the likelihood that these strategies could be continued and the individuals remain in unilateral control. Their strategies require secrecy if they are to succeed. But, as we find, the respondents in the conversation are busy filling up their own left-hand columns with comments predicting what is in the others' left-hand columns. Of course they too cover up, and cover up that they are covering up.

The next step is to discuss these diagnoses in the classroom. It is important for the group members to be given an opportunity to make their analysis of the comments and to do so publicly.

Box 6.2 is distributed to the class. They are given a few minutes to read it. The Faculty Member then says:

I should like to begin the discussion by asking you, what do you make of comments like these? What are you learning about these individuals? How do you evaluate these comments?

Participants typically said that the writers of these comments:

- were manipulative;
- were arrogant;
- were controlling;
- were defensive;
- were not listening;
- avoided conflict;
- believed they knew it; they were right.

These comments are written on the board. FM points out:

1. These reactions are primarily evaluations and attributions.
2. The responses are crafted in ways that are consistently the same as the crafting used in the left-hand columns of their own written cases submitted before arriving to the classroom.

3. The evaluations and attributions were crafted in ways that did not encourage inquiry into or testing up their validity.

FM asks for a discussion around such questions as:

1. How would they explain the patterns just pointed out?
2. How come the patterns in the cases that they wrote ahead of time and the patterns that they have just created in the classroom are similar?
3. How would they explain why the patterns they produced in class are similar to the patterns in their individual cases, yet they had concluded during the previous discussion that such patterns were counterproductive to learning?

The objective is to help the participants begin to see data suggesting that their responses appear programmed and resistant to change. If their responses do appear programmed and resistant to change, it suggests the hypothesis that they may be unaware not only of the counterproductive features of their spontaneous automatic skillful actions but of whatever causes them to be unaware. The objective is to help them to see that there is something going on that is fundamental and requires explanation. Moreover, whatever actions they design to correct these errors will have to take into account the fact that the errors were produced skillfully and that the actors were skillfully unaware of their skilled incompetence.

As these ideas begin to be considered, invariably some participants claim that all this may be true, but why the fuss? After all, they know not to say what is in their left-hand column, and certainly not to craft it as they had in their cases, or in the classroom. Their right-hand column would be more 'positive' for facilitating effective learning and action.

The FM then distributes a collage of examples that shows what a writer wrote in the left-hand column, and what he or she wrote that was said in the right-hand column (see Box 6.3).

The most frequent reactions of the participants are as follows:

1. In the left-hand column, thoughts are covered up. The cover-up is also covered up. Thus their predictions are confirmed.

Box 6.3. Thoughts and conversation

Left-hand column	Right-hand column
I'm going to get attacked straight out of the box at this meeting. They think that we are cowboys.	I'm so happy to meet you and get to know your organizations. I think we will have a great working relationship and can learn a lot from each other.
I need to help her learn how to step back and trust her stuff.	Your primary role as project manager is to set and manage client expectations...you have the responsibility to constantly monitor these things. If not, it can have detrimental longer-term effects on your team.
What a bunch of crap. I don't want to get drawn into this discussion of a past that I had nothing to do with.	I'd like you to know that I believe in open, direct communication and Joanne certainly does as well.
What the hell gave you authority to do that?	What did he say?
I know I'm smart. Some people appreciate this, but morons cannot. I'm under-appreciated.	That is surprising news to me. Irrespective of the projects I worked on, I think that I gave consistent output.
Did he say *our* plan? He must have meant his plan. Doesn't he know I disagree with his decision?	No problem. It seems like we're at a critical point.
Doesn't appear great for me at this point.	I agree that this deal has a tremendous upside.

Box 6.3. (*Continued*)

Left-hand column	Right-hand column
I'm being painted into a corner...I need to stall and regroup here.	Okay, but shouldn't we develop options...now?
She's thinking I'm snooping around for something.	How are you doing? What exactly are you doing on this project?...I hope that you are enjoying [your work].
Oh, no, she is now entirely visibly upset.	I want to also offer proactive, constructive feedback, which I hope you will take in the spirit in which it is intended.

However, what was missing before was a discussion of the consequences of such a strategy.

2. It is necessary to discuss the information in the left-hand column if valid communication is to occur. The strategies depicted in Box 6.3 simply postpone the inevitable.

3. The participants in the class and those depicted in the cases hold a Model I theory-in-use. They realize that they are covering up and they predict that others are doing the same.

4. These conditions often lead to the creation of self-fulfilling, self-sealing prophecies. This in turn can create the self-fueling generic syndrome of ineffective learning predicted by Model I theory-in-use.

What is missing in this learning experience is the explicit connection between these counterproductive consequences and organizational features such as organizational defensive routines. Often individuals provide in the classroom illustrations of how skilled incompetence and skilled unawareness created and then reinforced organizational defensive routines.

Such examples come out more powerfully if the audience, in whole or in part, comes from one organization. For example, the top executives of a very large accounting firm participated in a workshop. At one point, the managing partner observed that most of his fellow executives agreed that the counterproductive actions described in the cases occurred in the organization.

The managing partner agreed, and then added, 'if we examine our cases, they illustrate many of the problems that we spent several million dollars to reduce in our cultural change program'. The partner in charge of human resources pointed out that the managing partner had participated in the culture change workshops and evaluated them highly. The managing partner agreed that he did so, and that was what really concerned him.

THE ANDY CASE

The group described in this section was composed of thirty-four CEOs who were attending a three-day conference on leadership and learning. My component consisted of three two-hour sessions.

The participants read the 'Andy Case'[2] beforehand. It tells the story of how Andy failed to become a CEO in a company that hired him as the COO fully expecting that he would become the CEO. The case describes the authors' diagnosis of the errors Andy made that led to his demise (Ciampa and Watkins 1999). The authors state that, first of all, Andy did not learn enough about the organization. He failed to use the time before entry to jump-start his transition. Once aboard, he did not learn enough about the politics and culture of the company. When he did focus on learning, he concentrated on areas he already knew well and assumed that problems elsewhere could be resolved easily.

Second, he overemphasized action at the expense of understanding what it would take to make changes. He moved ahead with his agenda rather than combining what he believed to be

---

[2] This material draws heavily from Argyris (2002).

important with what was important to Ted (the CEO). In the process, he forgot who was the boss.

Third, Andy failed to motivate others, especially the senior managers in Manufacturing and Engineering, to abandon their comfortable habits and work patterns.

Fourth, he became isolated. Andy never built coalitions to support his efforts to transform the organization. He also misread existing coalitions, overvaluing his initial mandate from a key board member and failing to build a constructive working relationship with Ted.

Fifth, Andy did not manage himself well. His overconfident personality and lack of maturity caused him to make several bad judgements. A need to be seen as competent and in control blocked learning and prevented him from building supportive coalitions. His failure to manage stress, combined with his belief that his plan was correct, led him to blame others and kept him from recognizing warning signs or seeking advice (Ciampa and Watkins 1999: 9).

The FM introduced the case by stating that its purpose was to help participants become more aware of their effectiveness in helping others—in this case Andy—to become more effective leaders. The FM would role-play Andy, striving to make his behavior consistent with that of Andy in the case. If, at any time, people doubted the validity of his role-play, the FM asked that they please feel free to voice those beliefs.

The role-play by FM has two major components: (1) a genuine acknowledgment that he (Andy) did produce the aforementioned errors and (2) a genuine desire to learn not to repeat these errors in some future occasion. There are several reasons for these components. The first is to create a situation where the participants are not facing an 'Andy' who is strongly resistant to learning. This should help reduce the likelihood that, if the participants fail to help Andy, it is not caused primarily by Andy's resistance. The second is to use Andy's responses as explicit cues to the participants about which of their actions are helpful and which unhelpful.

Illustrations of What Happened

The following material is taken from transcripts of two sessions. Each session lasted about two hours. The first illustrates how Andy (role-played by FM) introduced his request for help and the dialogue that followed. The second session illustrates what happened when the FM asked the participants (P1, P2, and so on) to reflect on their experiences of the first session.

Session 1

Andy (role-played by FM) begins.

ANDY: You know folks, I was sucked into managing this company, especially during the courting period. They said they needed me, that I was the best candidate, and they promised that I would be the next executive. Now, I did some things wrong. And that is what I want to focus on. I do not want to repeat this experience again.

P1: I think you should have spent more time interviewing your direct reports, learning their skill sets.

ANDY: I have two reactions. One is that I did a lot of that. But, as I now see it, I probably behaved ineffectively during those interviews. I need to learn how I should behave during these sessions. What is it that you think I should have done more of?

P1: Show a simple force of strength ... develop measures for a baseline.

ANDY: No, I didn't do that. When I develop these measures, what do I do with them, do I give them to my immediate reports?

P1: Sure.

ANDY: Then what do I do?

P1: Measure their performance.

ANDY: And how would this help me to overcome the errors that I made?

P1: Well, you could then back up your decisions, for example, with firing the two executives, with quantifiable evidence.

The FM strives to identify any gaps and inconsistencies in P1's advice that are likely to make the advice—from Andy's perspective—less effective. For example, P1 does not specify the actual behaviors he has in mind when he advises Andy 'to interview', 'to learn', and 'to show a simple force of strength'.

P1 does not appear aware of these gaps. When 'Andy' asks him to make his advice more concrete, he remains at an abstract level. When Andy asks P1 how he believes his advice would help to overcome the errors that he made, P1 responds that he could fire the two executives with more legitimacy because he had quantifiable data to support such actions. Such interactions begin to build the case that Pl's actions are counterproductive to the very learning he advises Andy to produce, and that he is unaware of this counterproductiveness.

P2: You should have learned more about the workplace culture, especially his position. For example, learn more about the relationships these executives had with the CEO.
ANDY: Yeah, but the CEO, Ted, and the board kept telling me to focus on growth, growth, and growth. Also, they told me that this was a fat and happy organization. These attributes had to be changed...
P2: I would say that you can't believe everything you hear. You have to be careful; you can't be naive.
ANDY: I am not sure that I understand. Are you saying that I, Andy, am naive?
P2: Yes.
ANDY: Well, what is it that led you to this conclusion, that I am naive?
P2: Just because the CEO and board said that, it doesn't mean that you should accept it.
ANDY: Well, you are right. I was naive. I didn't think that he was playing games with me.

Andy defends his actions by placing the blame on the CEO and certain board members. For example, Andy states that he was acting to satisfy the CEO and the board's demands for growth and for changing the 'fat and happy' organization. P2 responds that Andy was being naive. Andy eventually admits that this may be true, but says he acted consistently with the demands that he be decisive and shake up the organization.

As the dialogue becomes repetitive, some members try a different strategy, namely, that Andy should have paid more attention to the organizational defenses and politics. This provided Andy the opportunity to project the blame onto the CEO and the board, saying that he acted in ways to fulfill his promises to both bodies. From Andy's perspective, he acted decisively.

Up to this point, we have a dialogue in which Andy expresses the view that the participants' advice was not helpful, and he defends his actions.

ANDY: I think you are telling me that I screwed up. It may be true—yes, it is true, but I don't find what corrective action that you believe I should take.

P3: Andy, if you could go back and do one thing differently, what would it be?

ANDY: I would not have taken the job. If I had known that Ted was not ready to give up the CEO position, I would never have taken the job. When a board member bangs his fist on the table while he is telling you to grow the company and another tells you the organization is fat and happy, and a third tells me explicitly that Ted is ready to leave, then I acted. I think some of you are saying I should have done a better job of due diligence. But how?

P3: You were making changes that harmed the organization.

ANDY: No, I don't believe that for a moment. I was helping the organization.

P3: Well then, I don't think that you will learn much from our trying to help you.

ANDY: Are you telling me that when I tell you what I honestly believe, you can conclude that I can't learn? What is the reasoning behind your conclusion?

The dialogue appears to be a recipe for creating feelings of frustration for both the advisers and the person being advised. If such feelings are brewing, they are not voiced. At some point, however, they are likely to surface, if no other reason than that Andy is evaluating the advice negatively and acting defensively. At the end of the P2 episode, for example, Andy states: 'I think you are telling me that I screwed up. It may be true... but I don't find what corrective action (you specify) that I should take.'

In P3's interventions, the advisers for the first time begin to focus on the ineffectiveness of their dialogue with Andy. The focus is upon what is going on in the room. Another feature is that P3's advice has been crafted in ways that make it easy for Andy to place the blame on others.

P4: I hear you using a lot of 'you' statements, but not a lot of 'I' statements. How does that help you to learn?

ANDY: I started this by saying that I needed help. So far the advice that I am getting tells me: 'You did create the errors (listed in the case material), you should start by correcting the errors', but how do I correct the errors? You tell me I should have gotten close to the CEO. I don't disagree with that. I'm just trying to figure out what I could have said.

P4: Ask the CEO, 'What do you do when you take care of these people that you say are fat and happy? What would you like to see done?'

ANDY: Well they told me, 'Energize these people, you run the show'.

Of interest is the fact that P4 is a faculty member of another CEO workshop designed to help the attendees become more effective leaders. One of the pieces of advice in his framework is that successful executives should first take responsibility for their actions (hence make more 'I' statements). Indeed, P4 showed a laminated card that included this advice. He used the card to help him craft advice. P4 said that this episode helped him to see that using the card as he did in fact did not help Andy to take on more responsibility for these actions. He also realized that he never thought of using the advice on the card to help him to see that the way he used the card actually helped Andy to reject the notion that he needed such advice.

P5: But you didn't go directly to the CEO and pose any difficult questions, such as 'If we move to replace these people who will support my actions?'

ANDY: You are right. It never dawned on me that they would not have supported me. Not with all the stuff they told me about being decisive and move the fat and happy organization. See, I said that I am going to show them what I can do.

P6: Maybe you should have studied the relationship between the CEO and his immediate reports more carefully.

ANDY: Yes, I think that the board told me that the CEO built the company, and there is a lot of loyalty to him and he feels a lot of loyalty to people. I also heard from the board that this is part of the problem. Remember, they told me that they had two or three good inside candidates, but they decided that they had to look outside.

P1: Andy, as I hear you, you decided that you didn't really need to hear from the old guard. It was like you made a decision that they were not going to change, and they had to go right from the beginning. What chance did they have under your regime to catch your vision and for you to bring them on board the team?

ANDY: Well, I admit I was biased against poor performance.

P8: Maybe you are trying to protect yourself.

ANDY: There is plenty of data that I protected myself and got myself in trouble. I want to learn how to not repeat that.

P9: Maybe you should have talked more openly and frequently with board members.

ANDY: Yes, what would I have said? And how do I deal with the CEO? What do I say?

The dialogue continues with escalating differences on behalf of all the participants: for example, P8 attributes simplistic solutions to Andy. Andy responds that he is getting simplistic advice. P8 counters that Andy seeks to protect himself. Andy replies that he wants to learn. P9 advises Andy to overcome his blind spots. Andy counters: 'How?'

When one participant's advice focused away from what is happening in the room, the FM decides it is time for him to intervene. Some of the criteria that he uses to justify doing so are as follows:

1. Data were generated to the effect that the advice was counterproductive and that the way it was crafted was also counterproductive.
2. Similarly, data were generated to the effect that Andy's actions led the advisers to attribute that Andy was closed.
3. Every time the advisers or Andy said something that focused on the here-and-now interaction, the group dealt with it by going back to the situation in the firm.

The FM concludes that these features have recurred so often that it is unlikely that the advisers or Andy would act in ways to interrupt or reduce the escalating counterproductive dialogue.

Session 2

The FM says, 'I should like to stop the role-play and ask us to do some reflecting on the past half hour or so. How do you feel about Andy? How does Andy feel about you?'

P1: He is a very frustrating individual. He says he wants to learn, but I doubt it. There is really no discussion, no sharing of ideas. He listens to a statement, then issues a defensive, 'you just don't understand'.

P2: I felt that Andy was waiting for the answer he wanted to hear. He kept saying to me that he was not open to our advice.

FM: Did you ever hear Andy say, 'I agree with your advice, but I don't know how to implement it?'

P2: Yes, he said that, but when he had an opportunity to react, he was not open to learning.

FM: What did Andy say that illustrates that he was closed?

P3: He kept changing the topic, blaming the board and the CEO.

P4: I am confused when he says to me that my advice is abstract, and therefore he cannot put it into practice.

FM: Did anyone hear someone say something like, 'Andy, if I am going to help you, I need to know more about what it is that you find unhelpful about my advice?' I do not recall hearing any such comment.

P5: To me, Andy was saying, 'yeah, that is a great idea', and then he dismissed it. He did not say, in effect, 'let's explore that further', it was a closed door.

FM: Perhaps Andy feels that way about you as consultants. He asks for your advice to be more concrete. He feels that this was not done.

The FM has two objectives during this second session. The first is to ask the group members to express publicly any feelings that they have about Andy during their role-play. The reactions are quick and strong.

- 'We doubt that Andy is genuinely interested in changing.'
- 'Andy espouses that he wants to learn, but he is closed to learning.'
- 'Andy seeks that advice that will make it possible for him to blame the others.'
- 'Andy seeks absolute control of the situation.'

The second objective is to use their replies to help the group members begin to examine the extent to which they have some responsibility for the frustrations they have experienced, such as placing all the blame for their ineffectiveness with Andy upon Andy. For example, after several evaluations and attributions that Andy is closed to learning, the FM asks if anyone has heard Andy say that he agreed with their advice, but did not know how to implement it. The group members responded by blaming Andy. Andy, in turn, responded to their help primarily by blaming the board and the CEO for his troubles. The FM points out that they appear to be dealing with their own failures by blaming Andy. Andy dealt with his failures by blaming the CEO and the board. They have been dealing with Andy in the same way that they criticized him for.

A second line of intervention with Andy could have been to examine his claim that their advice was abstract. No one responded to the criticisms by saying that it was not their intention to be unhelpful about their advice, or about the way that they crafted the advice. The group members agreed that no one made such inquiries, but the reason they gave for this was that Andy was closed.

These replies illustrate features of defensive reasoning. They begin with the premise that Andy was wrong when he claimed that the group's advice was abstract and unhelpful. When asked what led them not to test this conclusion, they responded, in effect, that there was 'not much sense in doing so because Andy was closed'. This is not a valid test of their claim that Andy was closed to learning, because the claim was part of their premise.

FM: May I ask, how do you think Andy feels about us?

P7: He is a victim.

P8: Not understood.

FM: And that is what Andy said about the board members and the CEO. They didn't understand him, that he was a victim, etc. So, as Andy, I am trying to figure out how I am going to get the help that I need.

P9: I go back to an earlier remark. What Andy needs is quantifiable information [that could be used to back up his firing].

P10: My feeling is that I can't offer anything to this guy that will work.

FM: May I reflect on what is being said to Andy? Andy, I tried to give you helpful advice; I did it with the best of intentions; I was immediately told that it wouldn't work, I tried to figure out why it would not work, you told me that you could not trust the CEO, you didn't give me any reason or didn't illustrate your attribution about the CEO, so Andy, I am left with the feeling that I know of no way that I can help you.

So when you ask for help, I say (to myself) not me. Is this a fair summary of your views and perhaps of others?

P10: You said it better than I did. (Two other voices—'Yes'.)

FM: This illustrates an important puzzle. What I said [above] came from comments made by members of this class. You know what to say, but you do not say it. How come?

Before we return to this puzzle, the FM notes a pattern in the actions of the members with Andy, that is, the dialogue took on the features of escalating errors and defensiveness, which became self-reinforcing and self-sealing. These features did not help to produce effective learning on anybody's part. Moreover, the features were kept private and unvoiced until the frustration became intolerable and the FM intervened to make all this discussable.

This pattern has been found frequently. We have labeled it as a generic counterproductive anti-learning pattern that occurs when human beings are trying to solve problems that are potentially or actually embarrassing, or threatening to their sense of competence in solving such problems (Argyris 1993; Argyris and Schön 1996).

A Theory of Action Perspective on the Andy Case

The Andy Case describes the errors he made that led to his demise. The participants see the source of his errors as a lack of knowledge and skills: for example, Andy did not deal effectively with politics, culture, and motivating people. But Andy made it clear he had become aware of his errors and was seeking help in reducing his blindness and increasing his skills. The first questions that arise are: 'How come Andy was so blind?' and 'how do we explain his lack of skills?'

Let us begin with Andy's beliefs about effective leadership behavior. Andy gives us many cues about his beliefs: for example, to be an effective leader:

- be action-oriented, that is, make getting the job done a very high priority. Give of yourself for the sake of the organization;
- hire managers who hold the same beliefs and degree of commitment;

- reward such managers; and
- reduce the barriers that are obstacles to the aforementioned; for example, try to help individuals whose performance is poor or mediocre to improve. If they do not improve, remove them. It is not fair to saddle good performers with poor performers.

Three important features characterize these beliefs. First, the beliefs take the form of causal claims. Andy claims that, if he behaves consistently with each belief, then he will be an effective leader. The second feature is that the causal claims form a moral basis for effective leadership. For example, Andy values personal responsibility, tough performance standards, and being action-oriented. The third feature is that the claims are crafted in ways such that their validity is difficult to test because they are stated in abstract terms. They do not specify the behavior required to implement them. For example, are there not conditions under which being focused primarily on the task might lead to ineffective leadership, or where hiring managers who are like him could create a conformity-oriented culture that inhibits exploring significantly different ideas?

The next question is: 'To what extent do the CEO and the board members bear some responsibility for the problems?' They also held beliefs about what the company needed. Recall, for example, their call to:

- shake up the place;
- get rid of the complacency;
- transform the management mentality from 'fat and happy' to lean and tough; and
- focus on innovation.

Their beliefs are causal claims about the leadership the company requires to enhance its performance. Moreover, as in the case of Andy, their claims are stated in abstract terms.

We have identified two basic causes of the problems between Andy, Ted (the CEO), and the board. First, Andy's theory of effective leadership contains several important gaps. It spells out effective results as he defines them. It does not spell out how, if he acts according to his views of effective leadership, he might alienate key people and reduce the likelihood of getting the feedback he needs to become aware of counterproductive impact. Andy's theory of effective leadership does not spell out how to deal with those individuals who cannot meet his standards—other than getting them out of the way.

Ted and the board members' view of effective action specified the results they wanted for the organization; however, they failed to make explicit the extent that they would tolerate Andy (or anyone else) acting as he did. Nor did they spell out what they knew at the outset, namely, that their strategy for dealing with differences would be to bypass the differences and cover up that bypass. As was true for Andy, their position on how to reduce any barriers to the achievement of their goals by Andy's (or anyone else's) ineffective actions was to ask him to leave. As in the case of Andy, the CEO and board members were unaware, and unaware that they were unaware, due to skillful incompetence. They recommended the following:

- help Andy make explicit his views about effective leadership and then help him to identify any inconsistencies in these views;
- help Andy to specify the features, if any, of his theory of effective leadership that inform him about how to deal with these inconsistencies so that they do minimal damage; and
- help Andy to specify the features of his theory of effective leadership that inform him about how to deal with his own and others' actions that are self-protective and counterproductive to learning.

It is fair to conclude that the participants in the class were not effective in implementing their recommendations. In this connection, recall that Andy kept telling the participants their advice was not helpful because it was abstract and did not contain advice about how to implement it. Moreover, in all cases when Andy voiced this complaint, the CEOs either blamed him for not understanding them or ignored him.

The FM stopped role-playing and asked the participants how effective they felt they were in helping Andy. All who spoke agreed that they were not effective. The participants explained their failure by blaming Andy. During the role-play Andy frequently blamed the participants.

If we step back and look at the entire case discussion, we find that:

- Andy was ineffective as a COO in the company;
- Ted and the board members were ineffective in dealing with Andy;
- the participants in the class were ineffective in helping Andy; and
- Andy was ineffective in helping the participants provide him with the advice that he needed.

Thus we see that interactions between Andy, Ted, and the board, Andy and the class, and the class with Andy created conditions that were not only counterproductive to learning but also were self-reinforcing and self-fueling of this lack of learning.

The Andy Case as a Quasi-Experiment

Campbell and Stanley (1963: 224) define an experiment as 'any experimenter-controlled event or "treatment" in the lives of respondents where probable consequences can be empirically assessed'. I should like to show that the 'Andy Case' learning experience could be used to test features of the theory used to design the learning experience. Transforming the learning experience into a quasi-experiment requires some relatively simple and straightforward actions that I describe below, such as minimizing threats to internal validity.

Develop A Priori Hypotheses

The first requirement is to develop a priori hypotheses. The following are some examples of hypotheses:

1. To the extent that participants hold a Model I theory-in-use, they will produce actions that are consistent with that theory-in-use.

2. Under these conditions, the participants will not produce actions consistent with Model II theory-in-use, even if they espouse that theory.
3. Under these conditions, participants will be unaware of any discrepancies that they produce between their espoused theories and their theory-in-use while they are producing them.
4. If the participants become aware of the discrepancies, they will automatically and spontaneously blame others or the system in which they are embedded.

Recall that the theory-in-use is a causal design activated by actors that produce the actions that they intend. The design is programmed to produce these actions and no others. This means that we should not find exceptions to the predictions. As Lewin (1935) pointed out, one exception serves to disconfirm the hypothesis.

Creating Observable Categories Derived from the Theory

Using a Model I theory-in-use, we suggest that the three actions of advocating, evaluating, and attributing will be crafted in ways that do not include illustrations of their meaning, do not encourage inquiry into them, and do not encourage robust testing of the claims being made by the actors (see Box 1.1).

A Model II crafting would include illustrations, would encourage inquiry, and would encourage testing. A somewhat more complicated scoring procedure has been found to have a respectable degree of inter-observable ratings (Argyris 1965).

Time-Series Observations

Campbell and Stanley (1963) advise that a time series of observations will enhance the credibility of the findings. The observers or analysts scoring the participants' actions in fifteen-minute (or longer) segments can fulfill this requirement. Thus, instead of the one-shot feature of the Andy Case as presented in this chapter, it is a relatively straightforward procedure to strengthen the claims significantly by reducing these threats to internal validity with the use of a time-series design.

Independent Measures of Model I and II Actions

The above hypotheses conjecture that the participants hold a Model I theory-in-use. It is necessary to have a measure of the degree of 'Model Oneness' of each participant before he or she enters the classroom.

Measures such as these have been obtained by observing the participants in their home settings (Argyris 1993; Argyris and Schön 1996). We used the left-hand/right-hand case methodology to assess the participants' theory-in-use in the home setting.

Box 6.4. Scoring conversation

Conversation	Scored as
'Andy, you failed. You mis-assessed the situation.'	Negative evaluation. No illustration, no encouragement of inquiry, or testing.
'Andy, you are very good at talking, but not at all good at listening.'	Same as above.
'Andy, you should study the culture carefully, especially how the CEO communicates with the organization.'	Advocacy; no illustration, inquiry, or testing.
'You believe that you have a messianic right to organize, without contemplating the effect on others.'	Attribution; no illustration, inquiry, or testing.
'You have a strong need to be seen as competent and to be in control.'	Attribution; no illustration, inquiry, or testing.
'Concentrate on areas that you do not know well.'	Advocacy; no illustration, inquiry, or testing.

Before they arrive we ask the participants to complete a short case that illustrates an important challenge that the writer of the case is facing or is expecting to face.

The cases could be scored by the FM or by raters who were not participants in the learning experience. The latter provides an independent assessment that can be compared with the one made by the FM. An additional set of data can be obtained by asking the CEOs to score their own cases toward the end of the workshop. Indeed, learning to score their cases becomes an opportunity for them to learn to reflect thoughtfully on their actions.

The cases and the analysis of the transcripts from home meetings on everyday organizational issues are valuable in dealing with the possibility that the 'treatment' in the Andy Case session could either be the case by itself or the case and the FM. If the home cases indicate Model I theory-in-use, the claim that the Model I actions during the Andy Case are caused by the CEOs is then supported.

Random Assignment to Experimental and Comparison Group

Another challenge to threats of validity is to create control or, more accurately, comparison groups that do not receive the experimental treatment. This is even more effective if individuals can be assigned randomly and secretly to each type of group.

The requirement is difficult to fulfill because the human beings who attend the courses do so because they are promised, and they expect, that they will learn to increase their effectiveness. How do you lie to one group and cover up that you are doing so? How do you do this in a learning environment designed to reduce lying, cover-up, and cover-up of the cover-up?

Some strategies begin to approximate this requirement. For example, the FM used in the Andy Case may also be used in a primarily lecture-based session describing the theory-of-action approach. One could compare the home results with those at the lecture session in home meetings. One could also ask the participants to write left-hand or right-hand column cases that they believe illustrate how they implemented their learning in the home situation. These cases should show no change in theory-in-use, even if the participants claimed that they learned Model II and intended to use it.

Another possibility is to have the experimental group go through its re-education in a fish-bowl setting where a larger group observes but does not participate. Beer (2002) has used a version of this strategy, which, however, involves the onlookers in a separate session or in sessions with members of the experimental group.

Implications for Creating New Learning Experiences

All these considerations lead to the hypothesis that the programming and the skilled lack of awareness (when producing action) create the appearance that actions are 'wired-in'. This, in turn, suggests that the model in good currency about unfreezing the old, introducing the new, and freezing the new should not be taken to mean that Model I is permanently unfrozen and somehow eliminated. I cannot, to date, conceive of a process that 'unfreezes' some designs-in-use that are already programmed. I believe that a more accurate explanation will someday be shown to be that unfreezing means that individuals become aware of their skilled incompetence and skilled lack of awareness. A new process then accomplishes learning Model II. The result is that individuals have two theories-in-use stored in their heads. This provides human beings with two degrees of freedom in choosing how they will act. Model I, for example, may be preferred when learning single-loop skills that are part of the existing routines. Model II may be more appropriate for solving non-routine potentially or actually embarrassing problems. For example, a Model I production of the social virtues is quite different from a Model II production (see Box 1.1). Most human beings, as we have seen in Chapter 1, do not realize the differences.

A closing note. Fourteen advanced change professionals were sent, in advance, the Andy case to be discussed during a seminar that they had elected to attend. A new experimental feature was added. We sent the participants, in advance, the analysis of the CEO seminar as described above. They read the Andy case *and* the analysis before discussing the Andy case.

The three-hour discussion of the case was tape recorded with the approval of the participants. Two independent observers and myself agreed that this group had produced the same counterproductive consequences described in the CEO seminar (as well as in all the other seminars where the Andy Case has been used). Thus, having the analysis ahead of time did not appear to produce more positive learning outcomes.

We plan to repeat the experiment in several forthcoming seminars.

THE RICHARD CASE

Throughout[3] this book, I have emphasized the importance of the role that defensive and productive reasoning plays in informing action. Defensive reasoning, the hallmark of Model I, inhibits learning and is especially detrimental to double-loop learning. Productive reasoning in the arena of human interaction facilitates double-loop learning.

The story of the Richard Case is similar to the one about Tom in Chapter 2. Both professionals began a set of relationships with line managers intended to help them become more effective in combining business issues with human relations issues. In both cases, the workshops wore out their welcome with line managers. Richard and Tom diagnosed the line managers' reactions as indicating resistance to change and withdrawing their commitment to learning. The line managers explained their actions as sensible responses to workshops that were ineffective. They did not believe that the organizational development professionals had the knowhow or the skills to design and implement useful workshops. One

---

[3] This section borrows heavily from Argyris (1987). See also Argyris (1990a). For a different example, see Gold, Holman, and Thorpe (2002).

consequence was that the professionals accused the line managers of being two-faced. The line managers reacted by distancing themselves from the workshops.

In the cases of Tom and the three senior change professional workshops, the focus was largely on the Model I actions by the change professionals once the going got tough. In this case, I should like to show how defensive reasoning was a crucial factor in the creation of the generic counterproductive, self-sealing, anti-double-loop learning syndrome. I also focus on the reasoning process that I used to inquire about and understand Richard's reasoning processes. I hope that these descriptions will help researchers to better understand how productive reasoning can be used to help expose and reduce defensive reasoning. This, in turn, may help to form the basis of research on enhancing double-loop learning.

I begin with a definition of defensive and productive reasoning. The characteristics of defensive reasoning include the use of data that are difficult to accept as valid descriptions of the reality experienced by actors in the same context but with contradictory views. Inferences are tacit and often private. The conclusions are crafted in such ways that they are not publicly testable.

Productive reasoning begins with relatively directly observable data that are easily acceptable as valid descriptions of the reality the actors experience, yet they hold contradictory views of how to interpret them. The premises and inferences are made explicit. The conclusions are crafted in such ways that they are publicly testable.

The case comes from a seminar conducted by myself with twelve organizational development professionals. Each completed a left-hand/right-hand case illustrating a challenging and difficult situation they had recently experienced. Below I quote the questions and comments raised by myself and the other eleven members, and Richard's responses, followed by inferences I made during the conversation about Richard's action strategies and reasoning. All names, except mine, are pseudonyms.

Q: How certain were you by the time the session finished that you had explicit commitment (from your client)?

RICHARD: I think I had a commitment, but not an explicit one...He is fairly indirect in terms of making expectations explicit. Lots of politeness. Easing-in. He is a master at it.

Richard did not test this attribution about client commitment with the client. Richard appears to explain the reasoning behind not testing his attribution by creating another, namely, that the clients prefer to ease in.

Making the easing-in attribution about the client and acting consistently with it is itself an act of easing in. Thus, the attribution Richard makes about his client may also be made about him. Richard appears unaware of this possibility. How does he know the easing in he is attributing to the client is not partially caused by his own easing in?

Later:

Q: What was your reaction to his intended use of the video?
RICHARD: I am opposed to using a video in order to hook people into a vision in which they were not intimately involved [in creating].

How does he know the client intends to use the videotape to hook people in? How does he know that the use of a video tape must necessarily hook people in? Why cannot it be designed to get genuine involvement?

If he thinks a video can be used in a way that is constructive, what prevented Richard from pointing out the difficulties with the client's views and how they could be corrected?

Again, Richard appears to be making attributions about the client's intentions that he does not test.

Q: Do you have ideas as to how to construct a good tape?
RICHARD: I've never done this before so I do not know what a good tape would look like. I do not even know how his would look like.

How can he then be so certain that a video tape will be harmful?

RICHARD: What I do know is that if we have the right tape, everything will happen.

How would he know what is the right tape if he does not know what a good videotape would look like?

RICHARD: The tape must communicate the correct vision. I believe in the importance of having the right vision. I feel it in my bones and in my cells, but I do not know how to deliver it.

He believes strongly in the right vision. What leads him to believe so strongly? He feels it but is equally clear that he could not produce the right vision.

What is the nature of his knowing? What prevents him from communicating it to his client?

Q: Have you told the client that you oppose video tape as an exclusive media?

What prevented him from testing the attribution with the client?

RICHARD: I think I've said it to him perhaps not in so many words. I do not know whether he buys that idea.

A repeat of the easing-in strategy.

RICHARD: I'm not sure that he would not be happy if we produced a tape that his staff could use to indoctrinate lots of people.

Again, what prevented him from testing the attribution?

Richard's Reasoning: Reflection I

Richard makes attributions about the clients' intentions that he does not test. Richard is unable to present the data in order to illustrate, nor is he able to make explicit, the chain of reasoning that has led to his attributions about the client.

Many of the attributions Richard makes about the client can be made about Richard, who, however, seems unaware of this possibility.

Richard believes that having the 'right' vision is key to success, yet he cannot define the features of the right vision to his own satisfaction.

Richard judges the client's ideas about video tape as counterproductive, yet he cannot state what makes them counterproductive, nor does he discuss this with the client.

Richard has little hard data with which to develop his premises about the importance and the practical value of having a vision. He is unable to make explicit his reasoning that leads him to conclude that he has the better or the more complete vision.

We may conclude that Richard's conversation so far displays several patterns.

1. *Untested and untestable attributions about the client.* Yet the validity of his conversation and help are dependent on the attributions being valid.
2. *Inconsistencies and gaps.* Richard questions the effectiveness of easing-in yet does it himself. He laments clients' unawareness yet he is also unaware.
3. *Strategies of persuasion through ideology and faith.* For example, Richard is sure that it is possible to produce an effective videotape, yet he cannot describe its characteristics, nor has he ever seen one. Richard asks the client to have faith that with genuine participatory problem-solving a solution will be produced.

Richard's automatic reactions to the inconsistencies and gaps pointed out by his peers is a surprise. Instead of inquiring into the basis for his unawareness, Richard asserts that the problem would be resolved if the client and he engaged in a mutually productive problem-solving process.

Richard's responses to his peers include untested attributions, distancing himself from his own unawareness, and trying to persuade his peers to have faith that the problems could be solved by a genuine joint problem-solving process; a process that he has not yet been able to produce with the client. Richard deals with his peers with the same type of defensive reasoning he used with his client. Moreover, until now, he has acted as if this is not a problem about which he or they should be concerned.

Back to the Discussion

As the discussion continues, Richard's peers begin to question more actively the reasoning behind and the validity of his attributions. For example, one asks him what he means when he wrote, in his case, about the client 'That's what I was afraid of (about him)'.

RICHARD: Yes (but notice that I realized that my doubts may be unfair). You know why should I expect a left-brain analytically trained manager to have this [my] notion of vision and to be able to pick up on it like that quick in a conversation.

Richard 'explains' the client's 'inability to understand' Richard's view of vision by saying that the client was educated as an engineer and is left brain-dominated.

Note that Richard has presented no evidence that the client is unable to understand; no evidence that this particular engineer was dominated by the left brain; nor any evidence that no engineer who is left brain-dominated can understand his notion of vision.

RICHARD: I mean I really believe that. It took me a year and I still cannot articulate it well.

Richard makes private attributions about the client's inabilities to understand his view of vision yet Richard does not understand it well enough to articulate it to his own satisfaction. It is at least a plausible hypothesis that Richard's inarticulateness could be causally relevant to the client not understanding.

Richard's reasoning excludes him as a causal variable from the problem that he identifies and focuses on the client in ways difficult to test: he is left brain-dominated.

One of his peers questions Richard about some features of the reasoning identified above.

Q: It sounds like you're saying, well okay, this left-brained-trained manager doesn't know any better...so you chose to teach him...about what is a vision.

York St John University
Check-Out Receipt

Customer name: QUIROZ, CATALINA, BERTA

Title: Reasoning, learning, and action: individual and organizational
ID: 38025002431669
Due: 1/3/2014,23:59

Title: Reasons and rationalizations : the limits to organizational knowledge
ID: 38025005257863
Due: 1/3/2014,23:59

Total items: 2
01/02/2014 13:02
Checked out: 4
Overdue: 0
Hold requests: 0
Ready for pickup: 0

Tel: 01904 876700

RICHARD: Well, in a way, I was trying to back off and not be judgmental and kind of accept him where he is and you know I was there too not too long ago.

Instead of Richard exploring the possibility that he has prejudged the client as needing education, Richard 'explains' his action to educate the client as an act of acceptance and tolerance. He will educate the uneducated.

RICHARD: By backing off (I meant) that I realized that it was maybe unfair for him to understand it so quickly. Recognizing my own struggle to understand this concept, I realize that it is going to take some time.

Note the phrases 'in a way' and 'kind of accept him'. The questions arise: 'in what way?', 'what kind of acceptance?' I believe that, if Richard explained their meaning, he might begin to get insight into the gaps in his reasoning.

Richard implies that he understands the meaning of vision well enough to communicate it and/or teach it to clients. So far, he has not illustrated this capacity with the client or with his peers.

RICHARD: We're gonna have to work together for us to understand our meanings of the word (vision) and then to be able to engage in some kind of a mutual process around how are we going to do it together in this context.

Richard expects that through a mutual problem-solving process the client can be helped to see what he now does not see.

Richard's Reasoning: Reflection II

Richard continues all the defensive reasoning processes described in Reflection I and adds a few more.

Richard explains the client's difficulties in understanding Richard's meaning of vision by (1) attributing that he has difficulties, and (2) attributing the cause of the difficulties to the 'fact' that the client was educated as an engineer and is therefore left brain-dominated. Richard now assigns full causal responsibility to the client.

Richard explains his attempt to educate the client in Richard's meaning of vision as an act of tolerance and patience with the client's limits.

Two additional patterns in Richard's reasoning appear in this episode:

1. Richard reacts to the client's questioning of Richard's beliefs by seeing the doubts expressed as signs of the client's limitations.
2. Richard acts as if the vague language that he used to explain his actions (for example, 'kind of accept him') was clear. If Richard's language is vague and if he believes it is clear, then he must be unaware of its vagueness.

If we combine these two patterns with the three listed above, Richard's conversation intended to help the client (1) contains untested attributions, (2) contains inconsistencies and gaps, (3) relies on ideology and faith, (4) deflects client questions by blaming him for his 'ignorance,' and (5) uses language that is vague.

Richard was not aware of these features while he was producing them with the client. His automatic reactions to his peers as they point out these problems is to use the same five defensive reasoning and action strategies just described. However, as we shall see below, when his peers are able to present further data and to discuss the consequences of these five defensive reasoning and action strategies, Richard begins to see what his peers are trying to help him to learn.

There is a theory of intervention embedded in the five defensive reasoning and action strategies which is itself inconsistent and highly unlikely to be effective. For example, Richard is, in effect, maintaining the following:

1. Although I (Richard) cannot articulate my meaning of vision, I will educate the client in my meaning of vision by engaging with him in a mutual problem-solving process.
2. It is possible for me to create a mutual problem-solving process with a client who I consider to be unable to understand my

meaning of vision, who has had an education that causes important blind spots, and with whom I have never tested my attributions and indeed kept them secret.

3. It is possible for me to hide my untested negative attributions from the client so that they do not inhibit creating a mutual problem-solving process.

Back to the Discussion

When Richard denies his peers' attributions that he was communicating to the client that his (Richard's) vision was better, several of his peers question him closely by referring to the dialogue Richard wrote in his case. Richard finally says:

I guess I did back off when I said okay, you've got one meaning for the term vision.

But you haven't got the one that I want you to get.

[Your understanding] is the commonly accepted meaning of the term. It is, however, *wrong*. (Richard's emphasis)

Richard is surprised by what he identifies as a slip. There is a silence, which is broken by laughter. Then he says 'It's the unenlightened term' and laughs. His peers join in the laughter and add terms like 'The unwashed version', 'the left-lane definition', each accompanied by heavy laughter.

RICHARD: I realize that I may come across (that my version is better than his) but I really do believe that we need both.
CHRIS: Could you illustrate in the case where you say this?

Richard scans his case and nods his head negatively.

At one point in the conversation, I role-played a supportive client interacting with Richard.

CHRIS: Richard, it sounds to me as if you believe that if this company had the right vision, if it understood it, a lot of good things would follow.
RICHARD: That is essentially correct. Yes.
CHRIS: Could you tell me what is that vision.

RICHARD: No I can't. Because I do not know the vision for what the company ought to do. I do not believe there is one vision. (Visions vary at different levels of the organization.)

Later:

RICHARD: Once we are clear about the vision then I can help you find the appropriate people to discuss it and implement it.
CHRIS: And what is it that they will tell me?
RICHARD: A way of getting people involved in developing your vision.

I then turned to his peers and asked, 'What is your reaction?'

I wouldn't let you (Richard) operate on me.
I think you know more than you're telling me. If you read these (outsiders' stuff) then you must have some idea of what they would bring to the table.
Why do I need you? Are you the middle man in this relationship?

Later:

RICHARD: I have a very clear concept of what a vision is as a concept and as an outcome. I've seen visions work for individuals. What I have never seen or been part of is how do you do this with an organization. I've seen it work beautifully for individuals. I know it will work for organizations.
CHRIS: In what way?
RICHARD: It will provide a sense of purpose, a sense of clarity, a sense of direction, a sense of excitement, a sense of moving in a positive direction.

Richard's Reasoning: Reflection III

As I listen to Richard, the following questions come into my mind. What is Richard's view of when he knows when he knows something? How does he know he knows what a vision is if he cannot produce it? How does he know it will work for organizations as it does for individuals when he has never seen it work?

Richard assigns to the successful use of a successful concept of vision all the outcomes that he wishes he could help produce in the organization. The reasoning behind what he is saying is instructive. I (Richard) conclude that all the good outcomes I promise will occur although I have never seen or produced these outcomes. All I need to know is what is a successful concept of vision and a successful process to produce it. Yet I do not know either. The logic appears more consistent with magic than with mutual problem-solving.

What prevents Richard from admitting the gaps in his knowledge and, therefore, problem solving with the client? If we recall the early discussion of Richard's case, he acted toward the client as if he knew what the correct vision was and how to produce it.

Back to the Discussion

We now enter a new phase where his peers are more openly critical of Richard's intervention as illustrated in his case. The comments included the following evaluations:

- You focus on what client is missing and not on what he is saying.
- You identify gaps in client's thinking and then you back off.
- You focus heavily on making sure the client would succeed by making sure he understood your view that you never got around to a solution that was acceptable to both.
- You create, right from the beginning, a win/lose situation.

Each of these comments focuses on Richard's behavior and is easily illustrated by the speakers. In all cases Richard agrees. He stops the group to say that he is finding the feedback difficult to hear but very helpful. 'I see now that I made quite a few misses.'

Chris asks him to 'identify the misses that he has heard so far.'

Richard responds that he missed the following: (1) he did not understand his own meaning of vision; (2) he tried to coerce the client to buy into his (Richard's) version of vision; (3) he insisted that his meaning of vision was better, and (4) he did not help the client to clarify his vision.

Richard then stresses his gratitude by saying, 'This dialogue has been very helpful. It has helped me to clarify where the mismatches are right now between the client and myself'. He then reflects further.

RICHARD: (I now remember) that the client talked about the importance of visions before I did.

This provides some evidence that contradicts Richard's assertion that the client, being educated as a left-brain engineer, would naturally be uncomfortable with the concept of a vision.

RICHARD: My axe with the client was that he was using vision in a rather manipulative way to sell his ideas.

Richard uses his concept of vision to manipulate the client. For example: 'In a sense, I can now see that I am manipulating the client. I'm trying to parlay his notion of a vision into something bigger which I believe would be more beneficial to the organization.'
    Later:

Q: I was touched by your willingness to acknowledge that you do not know how [to define your wider view of vision]...But I also wonder if you are not angry at the clients who do not have a vision?
RICHARD: The word hostility doesn't feel right for me. Frustration maybe.
CHRIS: You may be correct. Is there a way that we can test the different views?

Is Richard suggesting that the criterion for validity of the question is whether it feels right? How can his ideas then be genuinely disconfirmed?

RICHARD: Test? What is there to test?
CHRIS: To test the extent to which anger may be relevant.

What is the reasoning process that leads Richard to say that there is no need for the test, and at the same time admit that he feels highly frustrated? Could not his feelings of frustration lead to distortions?

RICHARD: Well do we need to test it? I mean there is a lot of frustration for me around the topic. I have a lot of frustration about where our company is, and where we are going to come out.
CHRIS: Yes, and?
RICHARD: I think our ability to succeed has a lot to do with the ability of people who are in key leadership positions to be conceptual...round

complex situations... What frustrates me is the way the line managers handle complex, difficult situations. They analyze it and give it a quick and dirty, one, two, three answer...For example, I sent a memo [describes situation]. I received a typical (simplistic) answer. That's not really a good answer. I don't like it. I expect more from them.

Richard believes his success is dependent upon line executives being skilled at conceptualizing complex situations. Yet he does not appear, so far, to have such reasoning skills himself. For example, abstractions that are to be productive must be comprehensive yet explicitly connectable to a given situation. Richard cannot do it with his concept of vision.

We may now formulate the following diagnosis based on Richard's comments.

I believe that our company and OD people are in trouble if we do not become better conceptualizers of complexity.

- I cannot meet this standard in my own work.
- I do not seem to be able to create mutual problem-solving situations where we can produce new solutions.
- I get upset when the line sends me simplistic responses.
- I do not explore these responses with line, because it may upset them and I could get rejected.
- I try as diplomatically as I can to get them to see the gaps in their thinking and action but, being left-brain-dominated, they are unable to understand me.

As the other eleven professionals discussed their cases, they began to see that they too used defensive reasoning and that this led to activating the generic counterproductive anti-learning syndrome. As these patterns became increasingly clear the participants began to relate them to organizational consequences. For example, the participants pointed out that most of the line managers used a control orientation. They responded to 'get out the product'. They created crises to get the employees' attention. They focused on the 'quick fix' strategy.

The professionals acknowledged the importance of control. But they believed that the control should be less unilateral. They believed that the line managers should take on a stronger learning orientation. The professionals also acknowledged that there were built-in tensions between these approaches. They then began to generate a map of the behavioral systems created at the organizational level to deal with the tensions. The map helped them to make explicit the causes at the individual, group, and organizational levels that reinforced line's ambivalence to OD programs. This frustrated and angered the professionals (line was sneaky, irresponsible, lacked courage), which in turn caused the line managers to increase their mistrust of and disrespect for the competence of the professionals.

Organizational Interventions that Facilitate Double-Loop Learning

In this chapter, I present four illustrations of interventions in organizations. The first one describes how the 'responsibility virus' can be diagnosed at all levels of the organization, and the steps that can be taken to reduce its counterproductive consequences.

The second illustration describes diagnosing defensive reasoning and defensive routines in an organization that inhibited the effectiveness of the launching of new automobiles.

The third illustration is of a new organizational structure that, if executed properly, would reduce the incidence of many organizational defensive routines. The experience today is that indeed it does lead to positive consequences. However, the potential is limited because some of its features require the executives to use Model II theory-in-use.

The fourth illustration is of an intervention that began by helping a top management group to learn Model II, and of the organizational consequences.

THE RESPONSIBILITY VIRUS

Martin (2002), like Lewin, believes that the narrative approach is useful for understanding and enhancing effective action. He begins with narrative descriptions, then makes inferences from these descriptions to explain his observations (which he realizes are also inferences). Martin believes that his inferences ought to be subject to tests of validity. First, he takes the position that scholars are responsible for testing the validity of any claims that they make. Second, he is committed to producing actionable knowledge from which advice can be derived about effective action. He owes it to potential users to generate knowledge that they can use to take his advice seriously.

Martin's objective is to help create a more supportive world for learning and action, especially of the double-loop variety. Martin is explicitly normative and also prescriptive; he makes the claims of both perspectives subject to test, and his ultimate test for learning is effective action.

If the practitioners implement the propositions correctly, this prescriptive stance passes the validity test, if the consequences predicted by Martin occur. In order for practitioners to be able to produce the validity tests, they must know the ideas and be skillful at implementing them. Thus, in order to test the validity of his theories, Martin designs learning seminars where the ideas can be taught and the skills learned.

The design of such learning seminars requires the use of normative and prescriptive advice. For example, the participants have to examine their defensive reasoning, skilled incompetence, and skilled unawareness; they also have to examine the organizational defensive routines that exist in their organizations as well as their personal causal responsibility for creating and maintaining them.

Finally, in order for scholars to implement all this, they will not only have to be skillful at creating theories and using research methods that do not reinforce the defensive reasoning and defensive actions presently characteristic of their organizations; they will also need the skills to implement these actions when they act as the designers and implementers of their change seminars.

Martin begins by describing the dynamics of the responsibility virus, which is activated by failure or fear of failure. He reveals the causal process by which leaders typically become over-responsible and followers typically under-responsible. He shows how this leads to self-fulfilling and self-sealing processes; for example, when errors are committed, the leader feels confirmed in his belief that he must take charge, while subordinates feel confirmed in their belief that the leader will not change, and hence become passive, 'run silent, run deep', and hide the fact that they are doing so.

Martin models the over/under-responsibility process. In the over-responsibility phase, the leader assumes singular responsibility for success. This ensures actions such as battling hard despite the odds and ignoring warnings. The result is that he or she gets into trouble. In the under-responsibility phase, followers assume minimal responsibility for success; they focus on others' responsibility, not their own, and feel disempowered and vulnerable. These reactions strengthen the leader's over-responsibility strategies, which reactivate the over/under-responsibility cycle. Failure seems to beget failure.

Martin introduces several concepts to account for the over/under-responsibility cycle. He hypothesizes that the participants have a Model I theory-in-use. He describes how defensive reasoning, skilled incompetence, and skilled unawareness combine to produce the cycle. He then describes the consequences of such self-fueling, self-sealing processes for the participants and the organization; these include misunderstanding, mistrust, resentment, distancing, and hopelessness.

Martin then introduces the concept of the responsibility ladder to define the conditions under which human beings can increase or decrease the dysfunctional effects of the responsibility virus. He hypothesizes six key levels to one of which most people gravitate in most situations. The lowest level of responsibility, at rung number six, is to drop the problem on the other party's desk and indicate helplessness. Rung five on the responsibility ladder is to ask the other party to solve the problem, but make it clear you will watch and learn for the next time. Rung four is to describe the problem to the other party, and ask for specific help in structuring it. Rung three is to generate options for the other, and ask the other party to make a choice. Rung two is to provide options to the other party, along with one's own recommendations. Rung one is to consider options and make a decision, informing the other party subsequently.

An effective choice structuring process begins with framing the choice. Step two enlarges the number of positive options. Martin states that an option should be thought of as a narrative or scenario: a happy story that describes a positive outcome and is internally consistent. At the time its validity need not be tested.

Characterizing options as stories, group members explore possibilities. During step three the group specifies the conditions that need to be met in order for it to believe that the story is sound. Martin introduces another new concept, which he calls 'reverse engineering'. The strategy is to start with the assumption that the conclusion is valid, then fill in the logic and the data that would have to hold to bear out the assumption. It is this process that invites the expression of doubts and disagreements.

Each group member is asked to specify the conditions he or she feels are at least likely to hold true. Once key barrier conditions are identified, group members test them in ways that they find compelling. The ultimate goal is to use tests that also produce internal commitment to the choice by the members of the group. The tests can differ in their degree of rigor. Finally, make the choice. This is often the most difficult as it requires time and the proper conditions. The proper conditions for the sessions are defined by the concepts Martin uses to make analytic interpretations throughout his book, which then become the concepts used for enabling and producing choice structuring.

I close with a discussion of Martin's views on redefining leadership and followership, which provides a contrast with Grint's study. Both require a redefinition of leadership and followership, where followership has a more powerful role than is described in the literature. Martin's perspective fills in the gaps and corrects the inconsistencies in Grint's presentation.

The heroic definition of leadership associated with images in books and movies leads directly to the responsibility virus. We need a new definition of leadership that inoculates us against the virus rather than contributing to it. The first step is to see leaders not as making unilateral and tacit decisions on the sharing of responsibility, but as establishing their own and others' responsibility through open dialogue. Second, the redefinition doesn't view the leader as one who heroically takes charge, but rather as one who seeks to match capabilities and responsibilities for both himself/herself and others. A leader may indeed end up with a greater share of responsibility, but that share solely reflects his or her greater capability.

The redefined leader makes his or her reasoning explicit and invites contrary views on the appropriateness of the level of responsibility chosen. Thus, the apportionment of responsibility moves from the implicit and undiscussable to the open and very discussable. Finally, in assuming accountability for performance, leaders set standards that stretch capabilities but don't obviously outstrip them, and make performance against those standards subject to public testing that extends well beyond the leader's own private assessment.

With respect to others, it is important for a leader to set responsibilities high so as to encourage growth. For the redefined leader, sharing responsibility is not a zero-sum game. Eliminating a leader's over-responsibility and followers' under-responsibility enables both parties to test and build their skills, thereby advancing both their individual capabilities and the capabilities of the entire organization.

Regardless of how well we apportion responsibility, failure will happen, either because we erred in assigning responsibility or because one of the parties did a bad job, or just because luck turned bad. In the traditional definition of leadership, the heroic leader jumps in at that point, takes charge, and fixes things. By contrast, the redefined leader jointly explores mutual responsibility for the failure, shares responsibility for the diagnosis, and works together to redesign roles and responsibilities.

A productive follower seeks to set his or her level of responsibility not unilaterally but in conversation with the leader. In considering the appropriate level of responsibility, we make our reasoning explicit and invite contrary views. In accepting accountability for performance, we seek standards that stretch our capabilities, as well as public tests of performance. Redefined followers seek to set high standards for responsibility in relation to the leader. They must hold the leader accountable for setting out his responsibility at a level consistent with capabilities.

In sum, Martin embeds his work in a narrative approach, as follows:

1. Analytical and poetic interpretations cannot be separated. Those who produce the stories ought to learn how to be skilled at analytical interpretations, indeed for use online. This is how they become reflective practitioners. Those who analyze the stories use the same methodology. Poetic and analytical interpretations are subject to robust tests of truth and validity. It is this requirement that is the basis for my critique below of Bruner's distinction between the logico-deductive and narrative approaches.

2. The concepts used to organize and causally explain the events intended to describe the universe 'as is' are used to create new universes for double-loop learning. They are also used to prescribe how to move from here to there.

3. The concepts used to understand and explain are the same concepts used to create the learning environments required to produce the new universe. They are the basis for the re-education and redesign of organizations.

4. Those who have learned the new concepts and skills can also use them to educate participants in their organizational settings. The learners become the educators and agents for change. This helps to assure that the new solutions will not only be produced but will persist.

5. Helping human beings to realize the discrepancy between their espoused theories and their theories-in-use and to overcome them requires a closer relationship between the scholar–consultant and those being helped. People are more likely to learn through stories, especially if the learning process they use is intended to help them produce more effective double-loop learning.

THE CAR LAUNCH

The story of the *Car Launch* (Roth and Kleiner 2000) is told with two purposes in mind. The first is to describe an intervention intended to enhance the competence of an organization in creating and implementing innovations. The description is in the form of a learning history of the events as organized and narrated by the authors.

The second purpose is to encourage the use of the learning history on the part of executives, change professionals, and students to help them reflect on their own thinking about innovation in organizations. The first purpose tells a story about the intervention and its effectiveness; the second purpose invites individuals to use the story to learn about their thinking and acting. The major portion of the book is about the first purpose.

The key features of the learning history are as follows:

1. *Descriptions, as organized by the narrative, of the sequence of events carried out by the participants.* The narrators' descriptions contain many quotations from the participants that provide the readers with insights into the reasoning behind the actions taken by the participants.

2. *Descriptions of how the interveners (primarily from within the organization) developed a strategy for double-loop learning and change.* Included in the descriptions are several 'change techniques' and models intended to help the participants get from here to there. Some of the change techniques came from the existing literature while others were developed by the participants themselves.

3. *Descriptions of the intense personal and emotional interactions that occurred as the participants learned about such features as their defensive reasoning, skilled incompetence, skilled unawareness, and organizational defensive routines.*

4. *Descriptions throughout the story about their fundamental assumptions and methods in telling the story.* For example, the authors were clear that the creators of the change program

intended to produce new knowledge about creating effective innovations. The creators were also centrally concerned about producing knowledge that could be used by others attempting double-loop interventions. The ultimate purpose of learning was effective action. Understanding and explaining were penultimate purposes all in the service of effective double-loop changes.

How to Read a Learning History

The authors identify themes that illustrate the underlying significance of their project. Each theme is told in the form of a 'jointly told tale', separating the authors' comments from those of the participants. There are four different types of materials.

The format is to portray the project as the participants experience it in such a manner that the readers can draw their own conclusions. The attempt is to make the 'sense-making process' visible. The reports include what the people did, how they interpreted events around them, and the reasoning behind their actions.

The six themes identified by the authors were as follows:

1. Hard results, soft concerns: did increase in openness and trust produce better business results?
2. Setting an example of non-authoritarian leadership: did the more participatory leadership styles learned by the project leaders produce more effective problem-solving and commitment to decisions made?
3. Introductory 'learning labs': to what extent did the learning laboratories help to provide the participants with more effective leadership behaviors?
4. Combining engineering innovations and human relations: to what extent did the technologies such as the 'harmony buck' help engineers who rarely integrated their views develop a commitment to enquiry across engineers with a 'stove-pipe' mentality?

5. Partnership: to what extent did the partnerships created in the learning labs lead to benefits that the senior leaders did not predict or plan?
6. Process innovation in the context of a large organization: to what extent did the documented success at the local level lead to a greater degree of cooperation and support by the most senior executives in the corporation?

Some Key Learning Technologies: The Learning Laboratories

'Learning laboratory' is a term used for a workshop, often also called a 'managerial practice field,' where people come to develop new skills, cycling back and forth between study and practice. The practice field (or learning lab) seems separate at first from the work environment, but gradually its concepts and values become integrated into regular work issues and the day-to-day job setting. This makes learning labs different from training sessions, which take place off-site and 'teach' techniques that rarely get put into practice on the job... Participants learn new tools by applying them to the issues they face in their day-to-day jobs. [The learning] labs at AutoCo focused on skills of conversation, reflection, and systems thinking... The learning labs at AutoCo alternated between conceptual sessions for learning new tools (of conversation and systemic thinking) and exercises for practising their use. These exercises were deliberately designed so that people could consider their own work issues with perspective that come from the deliberate telescoping of time and space. For example, a computer-based 'management flight simulator'... allowed participants to spend an afternoon working together through a product development process that would normally have required three to four years. (Roth and Kleiner 2000: 54–5)

Affinity Diagrams

Groups participated in many hours of discussions to diagnose the problems around new product development. The discussions resulted in documented conclusions such as (1) we have no vision, (2) we waste a lot of time, (3) we feel frustrated, (4) management requires detailed reports that are used to impress management rather than to identify the critical factors that require changes. Cooperation is low while not-hearing/not-understanding is high. The participants use the diagrams as a basis for formulating corrective action. As they try to produce solutions, they realize that the trust among them is low. The undiscussability of the low trust is high. The participants also come to realize that they require a way to map all the factors into a causal systemic analysis. Trust is important, but so is having a map to organize the causal interrelationships among the variables.

As the map is developed and as the possible solutions become apparent, the participants realize that they must create an atmosphere of trust and cooperation if the solutions are to be implemented effectively. The team developed some rules to guide their actions to increase trust and cooperation: for example, (1) a mandate that 'bearing bad tidings' would be safe, (2) ongoing sharing of information and perspective, (3) a culture of greater inclusiveness, (4) deliberate encouragement of informality and friendship, and (5) a mind-set that 'no one has all the answers'.

Reading the comments of the participants makes it clear that this learning did occur but at various speeds and depths of competence. It is also clear that those who were most heavily involved were also most heavily committed to transforming the rules from espoused theories to theories-in-use.

The settings in which the change was most effective and the learning was most powerful were those where (1) the core team meetings 'trickled down' the organization, (2) the program management demonstrated commitment by taking part in every learning lab, and (3) the launch and the change program managers supported each other.

The final results, according to the authors, were mixed. On the one hand, an impressive amount of quantitative versus qualitative data was collected that showed that the new program did lead to dramatic cuts in costs as well as in the time required to bring a new innovation to fruition.

The participants predicted that the financial results in particular would lead senior top management to accept the change program enthusiastically. To their surprise and dismay, this did not happen. The response of the senior top management was lukewarm, aptly illustrated by the top executive, who said, in effect, that the program results were interesting, but the participants must never lose sight of their 'real jobs' (Roth and Kleiner 2000: 95).

It became clear to the team that the top management never understood the impact of the learning labs on the new and more effective developmental progress: or, if it did, it did not believe such activities should become part of the 'real work' world. For example, the program manager, in a reversal of his traditional approach, told an executive vice-president candidly what to expect. The manager interpreted the executive vice-president's reaction as bad: 'he seemed to think that I was being uncooperative'. The program manager called a vice-president who became involved in the change efforts to ask for help. Several responded positively and in a way that they had never done before.

There are other examples where the project manager was helped but in a manner whereby the help given was covered up from the top, and the cover-up was covered up. Ironically, the project team was helped by the participants using the same cover-up tactics that it used at the outset of the entire program. Recall that it made a unilateral decision not to involve the senior management until the program generated results.

The team process leader concluded that they had not made a strong enough case. Worse yet, he concluded, the senior top management did not really understand the entire process. The mind-set of the top management toward these change programs had not changed. Why?

Why Did the Management Not Genuinely Commit to the Program?

In order to answer this question, I should like to review briefly some of the main findings. The team developed a diagnosis that included the following features: the behavior within each team and between teams was dysfunctional with respect to an effective, innovative process; the organizational defensive routines encouraged a 'smoke-stack' mentality, pressure to maintain the status quo, the sanctioned spinning of the truth, and the cover-up of the cover-up. In order to begin to reduce these features significantly, it was necessary to produce double-loop learning.

The facilitators created learning labs where the participants learned how they were creating the dysfunctional features that they decried. The facilitators created technologies through the use of which the participants could learn the new behaviors that would be required to reduce the dysfunctional features. As the participants became more aware, and as they learned the new behaviors, they were able to implement new norms that would facilitate trust and openness. For example, being a bearer of bad tidings became safe; no one was expected to have all the answers. Reflecting on their behavior to see how they inhibited innovation was accepted and rewarded; inclusiveness was required; no one was an outsider to his or her systemic problems.

The authors presented examples where the team members did, in fact, learn the new behaviors and generated a new climate of trust and openness within and between the teams that participated in the learning process. Inclusiveness, according to the authors, was genuinely developed.

The factors that contributed to organizational change included the trickling down of the new ideas and the new behavior as a result of the core team meetings. Many members of these core meetings returned to their respective departments to spread the learning, and also supported the diffusion of these ideas and behaviors by expanding the number of learning labs.

I return to the question of why the top management did not understand and did not enthusiastically commit to a program that, as indicated by measures they accepted, produced impressive results.

One important cause of the problem was the decision made by the program managers during an early strategy meeting to exclude a dialogue with the very top management until they could present to them enough statistical measures to make success difficult to deny and easy to accept. Excluding the very top management seemed to be puzzling since, as we have seen, one of the fundamental features of the program was that internal commitment was necessary and could be created only by inclusion.

The company program manager and the team manager agreed that the decision was inconsistent with the philosophy of the program, but was necessary to get the program under way. They explained that it was unlikely that the very top management would support this program, especially since it questioned many sacred assumptions held by the top. The meeting that was being proposed could be dangerous because the top could use it as an opportunity to cancel the program.

Recall that the findings summarized at the beginning of this session indicated that strong organizational defensive routines existed, especially at the top. Thus, the fears of the company managers were realistic. But does that mean that no discussions should occur in the advisory board to develop possible strategies? Perhaps such discussions could lead to the conclusion that the company managers were not only fearful of the top but were also doubtful of their competence where the top had greater power.

What if such meetings were held and the top management did cancel the program? What about the 'honest coercion' (as one manager called it) that was pressed upon the engineers to join up? What about the frustrations and bewilderment that they expressed about the 'selling promises' to the effect that the program could help make their work world more humane?

Also, did not the final results provide evidence that the top management was, as predicted, genuinely distanced from those below? Did not the top management's reaction help to guarantee a halt to further organizational learning? Moreover, did not the departure of the company program managers to create their own consulting firm provide further evidence that the firm was beyond help?

A more thorough discussion, however, might have produced a fall-back position of ambivalence and ambiguity. On the one hand, the story of *Car Launch* is about several courageous internal groups dedicated to changing the mind-sets of individuals and the defensive routines of the organization and to producing increasing trust, openness, and cooperation. They believed in the necessity of breaking down the counterproductive, rigid features of the bureaucracy. The participants were not neutral, nor did they believe in the value of learning separated from effective action.

On the other hand, the authors wrote the narrative with the intention of helping others to learn in contexts that were disconnected from action. They state that their aim is to educate, to better inform; *not* to sell, to persuade, to pressure others in one direction or another. They cite, at the outset, the words of James Carse (1986: 13) to the effect that storytellers do not intend to convert their listeners, to move them into territories of superior truth: storytelling does not succeed or fail.

How would the participants of the change program have reacted if they had been told, at the outset, that this was the ultimate objective of their efforts? Does not this stance provide support for the very top management's advice to the participants to get back to 'real life?' Would not this stance also provide support for the research efforts described at the outset that valued nontrivial change, yet did not make it part of the theory-in-use?

RE-CREATING THE ORGANIZATION

Ackoff's recent work on *Re-creating the Corporation* (1999) is an example of his longstanding commitment to design organizational structures (democratic hierarchy) and organizational policies (the internal labor market). He believes that, if such ideas are implemented effectively, the dysfunctionality of organizations being managed by Model I theories-in-use and organizational defensive routines would be reduced. Ackoff's designs are based on requirements such as the commitment to valid (or validatable) information, the creation of informed choices, and the importance of individuals, groups, and inter-groups facing up to personal causal responsibility.

Ackoff's structures and policies are enablers of Model II theories-in-use and organizational behavior systems that encourage good dialectic and learning. Ackoff is aware that solutions based on his ideas are more difficult to produce when they require double-loop learning, though he believes that the new structures will increase its legitimacy. He has worked with Donald Schön for many years and more recently with myself to explore these issues.

I begin my presentation with the concepts of democratic hierarchy (circular organization) and internal labor markets.

A Democratic Hierarchy

The features of a democratic hierarchy include the following:

1. Every manager is provided with a board that assists the unit in being fully responsible for its actions as well as participating in organizational decisions.
2. Each unit is allowed to implement any decisions that do not affect any other unit or the organization as a whole. Disagreements are resolved by going to the lowest-level board at which disagreeing units converge.
3. No manager makes decisions that have no effect on the organizational unit for which he or she is responsible but that do affect others.
4. Each board is responsible for seeing that none of its plans or policies conflicts with plans or policies made at relevant higher levels of the organization.
5. Each board has the responsibility for the quality of life in the level below it.
6. Subordinates on each board meet separately to formulate suggestions to the manager to whom they report about what the manager could do that would enable them to do a better job.
7. Each board has the authority to remove the manager. The board cannot fire a manager but is able to relocate him or her.
8. Boards operate by consensus, not majority or plurality rule.

Ackoff notes that, in order for these structural requirements to be implemented effectively, the implementers will have to become committed (1) to take full responsibility for their actions, (2) to show equal respect for all units regardless of their position in the hierarchy, (3) to be internally committed to the effective performance of their unit as well as its interdependent responsibility to the whole, and (4) to provide subordinates with the power to evaluate their superiors effectively, and superiors with the power to do the same with their subordinates. In order to implement these features, participants must be dedicated and skillful at producing valid information and knowledge, pay vigilant attention to producing informed choice, and take personal responsibility for implementing and monitoring the choices. These conditions, in turn, require the use of productive reasoning and the avoidance of defensive reasoning. All these behavioral strategies are consistent with a Model II.

Ackoff is aware that, in order to implement the democratic hierarchy, the participants will have to become aware of, and overcome, their predisposition to act consistently with Model I. For example, he states that the principal obstruction to adapting the circular organization or democratic hierarchy is the satisfaction that some managers derive from exercising authority over others and the conviction that unless they do so 'things would fall apart'. Doubting the ability of others to accept personal responsibility, as we have shown, is characteristic of Model I.

Ackoff credits Goggin (1974) with the original attempts at implementing an example of a democratic hierarchy that Goggin calls the Multi-Dimensional Structuring (MDS). Reading Goggin's description, one gets the impression that he worked hard at communicating the ideas and that the participants listened and were receptive. However, even when the participants said that they were committed to the new structures and even when the champion was the chairman of the board and chief executive officer, the degree of commitment and the degree of implementation varied. Goggin reports that the most difficult challenge was to change the mindset of the participants, along with their designs-in-use, to manage effectively. As I read Goggin, the majority of his subordinates used Model I mind-sets. This made the multidimensional structure puzzling to them. For example, they had learned that in order to be effective leaders they should be in unilateral control, they should be concerned about their particular unit, that it was top management's responsibility to focus on the organization as a whole, and that they should never be placed in a two-boss system.

Moreover, the basis for the commitment to MDS had to be internal (not simply that the CEO was championing it), freeloaders were no longer to be tolerated, and internal politics and empire building were no longer sanctioned. The frequent use of self-protection when dealing with failure and near misses was not needed, and a 'telling it like it is' mentality was to be rewarded. Resistance to implementing these ideas, reports Goggin, was strong. He advises other CEOs and their boards to exhibit patience. In his case, it took three to four years to develop a satisfactory implementation.

For example, Goggin reports defensive routines and defensive reasoning among his subordinates.But he did not explore the causes of the defensive routines that he called resistance. Perhaps he hoped that these would be overcome as the people (1) fully understood the positive features of the multi-dimensional organization, (2) developed the necessary skills, and (3) reduced the organizational defenses. It is doubtful that these hopes would be realized if the subordinates did not become skillful at a theory-in-use that was consistent with Model II. As far as I can ascertain, they did not receive such re-education. Without such learning experiences it is not likely that they could produce the learning competencies required by the democratic hierarchy.

Internal Markets

A democratic hierarchy needs a supportive internal organizational environment. A market economy as defined by Ackoff emphasizes the importance of personal responsibility. For example, every unit is either a profit center or a cost center; every unit should be managed by criteria that are transparent and validly connectable to performance; every unit should have the freedom to buy any service or product it wants from whatever source it wants, and a similar freedom in selling its product. An internal market economy facilitates the goal for which the manager of a profit center has the responsibility and the opportunity to manage a unit that is semi-autonomous. The managers and their units are held responsible for acquiring whatever resources, especially information and knowledge, are required for effective performance. The internal market economy discourages the Model I concept of power-over and encourages the power-to that is more consistent with Model II. Ackoff (1999: 222) makes it clear that the implementation of an internal market economy 'is not a task that attracts the fainthearted; it requires considerable courage'. The organizational defensive routines will have to be exposed and reduced. If they are not, these underground defensive activities will await a future date to become activated.

Halal's (1986) description of implementing internal markets that illustrate the existence of defensive reasoning and actions on the part of he participants.

Halal claims, in effect:

- if internal enterprises (each unit is treated as a separate company) are created that are free to manage their own operations and resources;
- if they reward performances, challenge, and innovation rather than supervision, security, and bureaucracy;
- then entrepreneurial, self-organizing, creative actions as well as mutual problem-solving and collaborative synergy will result.

Halal then points out that internal markets are necessary but not sufficient for ensuring effective management; additional factors such as inspiring and strong leadership are required. Unfortunately, these factors are not defined as specific components of internal markets. Halal helps us to implement internal markets but not the behavioral features that are necessary for effective implementation.

The positive features of the internal market include a fundamental assumption that, if the focus of control is moved out of the hands of top executives and shared by those who are actually involved, then performance will be more effective; moreover, resistance to change will be reduced because the changes originate from those who participate in it, giving them a sense of ownership of and mastery over their future. The task of leaders is to direct attention away from themselves and onto their followers.

These claims assume that if, through appropriate structures such as internal markets, human beings are provided the above 'enablers' and wish to act accordingly, then the positive consequences will follow. The claims also assume that inner contradictions and their defensive consequences do not exist or, if they do, they can be overpowered by the structural conditions.

The claim that when groups are given genuine control over their destiny they will produce more effective performance is, as we have seen, optimistic. These positive consequences are not likely to occur if the tasks are potentially embarrassing or threatening. In a recent study, Barker (1999) found that groups could use their power to act in a Model I manner when members did not behave as they were expected to.

Ackoff states: '[If] an organization is to be effective, it must transform itself... *mere reform will not to do... a radical change in the structure and functioning of an organization*' is necessary for transformational change' (1999: 105; emphasis is his). I agree, and suggest that is why education in Model II theories-in-use is necessary.

Learning

'To learn is to acquire information, knowledge, understanding, or wisdom' (Ackoff 1999:164). Adaptation is learning that is required to maintain and increase efficiency and effectiveness. In order for organizations to learn, they require a relatively complete learning system that detects errors, diagnoses them, and presents corrective actions. Learning systems require information, knowledge, and understanding. The focus is upon the context of decision-making because that is the only context in which learning can take place.

Ackoff describes, in more detail than can be included here, a model of an organizational learning, adaptation, and management system (1999: 167). Some of the key components of the organizational learning systems are as follows:

1. Generate data, information, knowledge, or understanding about the behavior of the organization being managed and its environment. The focus is on behavior that is related to the flow of work in the organization.
2. Messages are filtered for relevance and condensed to minimize time required. Avoid overload of communications.
3. If information, knowledge, or understanding is incomplete or not understandable, generate new requests. Continue until the information and understanding are adequate.
4. Decisions include instructions and motivational messages.
5. Create a decision record.
6. Monitor the implementation of the decision.

Instructions also exist on what actions to take if errors are identified. For example:

1. If information, knowledge, or understanding is in error, change the support system so that error is not repeated.
2. If the decision-making is faulty, change the decision-making process.
3. If the decision-making is correct but the implementation is faulty, change the behavior of those in the organization who are responsible for implementing the communication of the instructions and motivational messages.

To the extent that the individuals have the skills to produce these requirements for learning them, they will be able to produce effective learning. The problems arise when the requirements demand Model II theories-in-use consistent with the good dialectic. This is confirmed by Ackoff, Goggin, and Halal. For example, these challenges existed for Goggin even though he was the chairman of the board and CEO, but he championed the idea with enthusiasm and commitment and his subordinates agreed that his ideas about organizational structure made good sense. They had no problem with the idea as enablers; but they did have difficulty implementing them.

This suggests an experiment in an organization where the intervention is designed, at the outset, to combine the democratic hierarchy and double-loop learning. Ackoff and I are exploring several opportunities.

I turn to an example of an intervention designed to create an organization that sought to become skillful at double-loop learning. Our hope is that someday Ackoff and I will be able to report on an intervention that was designed, at the outset, to integrate the concepts of the democratic hierarchy and double-loop learning.

AN ORGANIZATIONAL INTERVENTION

In the previous cases, features of a process of teaching and research were illustrated in which individuals and groups were helped to explore the transition from Model I to Model II. In this example, a more comprehensive organizational orientation is described, aimed at helping the organization move from an Organization Model I (O-I) to an Organization Model II (O-II) learning system. The illustration represents only a partial description. (For a more complete description, see Argyris 1993 and Argyris and Schön 1996.)

The study was initiated because the directors, who were also the founders and owners of a management consulting firm, concluded that the firm could develop the negative internal characteristics they had so much disliked in the consulting firms they had left. They also concluded that these very characteristics could limit the quality of the consultancy they provided to clients, especially around issues that involved double-loop learning. The directors believed that double-loop learning would be increasingly important if they were to produce added value for their clients in the future. They also concluded that they were unlikely to provide such assistance if they did not manifest these learning competencies in managing their own internal activities, as well as those that bridged toward client organizations.

I began by holding a series of meetings with the directors in order to set the terms and chart the directions of the intervention. In this process the directors displayed an extremely strong internal commitment to learning. They made no attempts to place sole responsibility upon the intervener, water down his aspirations for change, or place direct or indirect constraints on what would be studied. The directors expressed support for eventual publication of the research, believing that a publication requirement would assist in producing a high-quality intervention.

Framing the Problem

The seven directors of the organization in this case study framed their initial problem in various ways. They said they wanted to create an organization capable of persistent double-loop learning, both within the organization and between itself and its clients. They also wanted to know how to reduce the 'politics' they thought inhibited their objective of building a genuine 'learning organization'. And they wanted to discover how to build an organization where double-loop learning not only occurred persistently, but did so under conditions of stress, embarrassment, or threat.

During his first interviews, the intervener tried to determine the extent to which the directors believed that counterproductive activities were occurring and their view of the organizational consequences of these activities. He also tried to discover the directors' causal explanations of these phenomena. As we shall see, most of their explanations were abstract and several stages removed from directly observable data, and were not testable because they were not rigorously connected to such data. For example, the directors' explanations included unillustrated attributions that 'people are not candid', 'group decision making at the top is poor', and 'coalitions exist that create rivalries'.

The intervener faced two major tasks. One was to provide a causal explanation that gave a coherent, holistic, testable account of the directors' many multi-leveled, disconnected explanations that could also be used for designing and executing the intervention program. In turn, the intervention program and its consequences could provide opportunities for further tests of the explanation.

The second task was to develop generalizations about how to interrupt and reduce organizational defensive routines and skilled incompetence, and then to help the directors (and, later, consultants at all levels of the organization) acquire the skills necessary to spread the learning throughout the organization in such a way that it not only persisted but also grew and deepened.

I interviewed the directors to learn their respective causal explanations of the problems they considered important. These explanations were mainly representative of the directors' espoused theories. These theories and observations of actual behavior were then translated into descriptions of individual and organizational theories of action, at the levels of both espoused theory and theory-in-use. Next, an organizational map was developed to illustrate the organization's theory-in-use for dealing with the issue of organizational politics. This map made explicit the organizational defensive pattern on this issue, a pattern that partially explains the existence of activities counterproductive to learning.

The map was fed back to the directors. One purpose of the feedback was to assess the degree to which the directors confirmed or disconfirmed features of the map or, indeed, the map as a whole. I placed a heavy emphasis on encouraging attempts to disconfirm the map for two reasons. As a researcher, I wanted to encourage the toughest possible tests of the ideas; as an intervener, he knew that the design and implementation of the change program would greatly depend on the explanatory map. If the map was faulty, I wanted to know early so that I could correct it, and he did not want the directors to withhold their doubts only to raise them after the change activities began.

Purposes of the Feedback Session

The first feedback session had six purposes:

(1) to describe to the directors what had been learned from the interviews and the early observations of their meetings;

(2) to encourage any disconfirmation or confirmation of the findings;

(3) to start building an incremental relationship of trust among the directors and between the directors and the intervener;

(4) to plan actions that would correct whichever counterproductive activities the directors chose to correct;

(5) to plan the intervention steps required to implement these corrections; and

(6) to conduct planning in ways that would facilitate the directors' internal commitment to further steps in the intervention. This internal commitment would mean that the directors would be motivated to implement the changes, because doing so would be intrinsically rewarding.

The Feedback Process

Whatever methods are used to diagnose an organizational situation and whatever data are collected, four features are important to an effective feedback process.

1. The material should be organized to describe the variables that cause the functional and dysfunctional activities of the group being studied. The basic criterion for separating functional from dysfunctional activities is the degree to which each activity facilitates or inhibits the detection and correction of important errors in the production of innovations within the group.

2. The variables should be organized into a pattern that shows explicitly how the variables evolved and how their mutual reinforcement leads to the persistence of the pattern. The

description of the pattern should enable the prediction of its consequences.

3. The pattern should make explicit the likely personal responsibility of each director in causing and maintaining the pattern.

4. The pattern should be presented in the form of an action map, and that map should present the data in ways that allow the participants to derive the inferences that permit comprehensive understanding as well as those that illuminate each unique individual case. The data must also be conducive to generalizing about the present and the future. In addition to providing information for all of these analyses, the map should be generalizable (by reflective transfer) beyond the group to include other parts of the organization as well as individuals in other organizations.

The feedback process should help to provide a more holistic and systemic picture of organizational reality. This picture should be holistic in the sense that it covers a bigger slice of reality than the existing views of individuals or sub-groups do; it should be more systemic in the sense that it makes explicit the interdependencies that result in a self-maintaining pattern.

Tests of Validity

An action map constructed for a feedback session is primarily a representation of actions, strategies, consequences, governing conditions, and the feedback and feed-through mechanisms that relate these phenomena to one another in a persistent pattern. Action maps are, in effect, hypotheses about what drives learning and anti-learning activities within the organization. Therefore, all action maps have to be tested as frequently and as completely as possible.

There are several strategies that may be used to test a map's validity. The first is to show it to the participants to discover which features they confirm or disconfirm. However, the researcher should be aware that certain conditions predispose individuals to provide too easy confirmation. We have found that participants are too willing to confirm a map if they believe the result is only research knowledge. They are unwilling to put themselves, their peers, and their organization on the line for the sake of producing maps for scholars to publish in professional journals. This is not to say that they would confirm glaring errors; if the error is glaring, it is unlikely that they risk much by disconfirming it. But in our experience, they are reluctant to disconfirm when opinions vary widely, when topics are 'hot', and when topics are encased in longstanding organizational defensive routines—precisely the conditions under which researchers would seek a healthy debate. Conversely, if the participants have agreed at the outset that the research will include intervening in order to change the status quo and open up the Pandora's box they have feared, as well as undermining the defenses they have created to protect themselves, then they are more likely to reveal their doubts about the map.

A second strategy to test the validity of a map is to make predictions based on it. An especially robust test will occur when the researcher's predictions are made known to the participants, the participants disagree with the predictions, and yet the researcher turns out to be correct. For example, the map presented to the directors described how organizational politics were created and maintained. The directors discussed the map in a lively session; some felt the session was so productive that they would be able to change their actions immediately. The intervener and his co-researchers predicted that they would not be able to do so. They were able to test this prediction because they observed and recorded several board meetings that took place after the feedback session but before the first two-day change sessions. An analysis of the tape recordings confirmed that the defensive routines described in the map were alive and well.

Such experiences raise questions about the common assertion that any intervention, including asking people to fill out instruments or to be observed, leads to changes. In our experience this assertion is likely to be true only when the changes are in action strategies rather than in values, that is, when they are related only to single-loop learning. It is possible, for example, to help an authoritarian, aggressive leader behave less aggressively, but that behavior often vanishes when the individual is exposed to embarrassing or threatening conditions. The moment the individual experiences moderate to high stress, he or she reverts to Model I theory-in-use and defensive reasoning, which the individual has never abandoned. Managerial gimmicks and fads are often based on behavioral changes that are not accompanied by changes in governing values.

A third testing strategy is to predict the likely consequences of attempts to change the status quo. These tests will be even more robust if the change requires altering what is taken for granted. The more one can specify ahead of time the conditions of change, the sequences of actions that do and do not lead to change, the individuals or groups that will learn faster, and the conditions under which this learning will occur, the more robust the test will be.

These specifications can be produced by designing re-educational experiences directly from the knowledge embedded in the map. For example, the intervener and his co-researchers could predict that the map they had created for the directors was not going to change unless the directors changed their Model I theories-in-use to the approximate features of Model II. In moving toward Model II, individuals would have to unfreeze Model I. The researchers could assess the degree to which each director (and, later, others) would unfreeze Model I and practice Model II. They could also make predictions about the likelihood that the directors would be able to effect non–trivial changes in organizational politics. Note that this does not mean that individuals in this situation have to get rid of their Model I skills, which may still be relevant for routine issues requiring only single-loop learning. Nor does it mean that all the new behavior produced will be a pure example of Model II. There will be many instances of hybrids of Models I and II as well as instances of pure Model I behavior. What the researchers will observe, if there is genuine movement toward Model II, is that individuals will recognize and reflect on their

Model I actions or will express discomfort about such actions without inhibiting their learning.

Discussions During the Feedback Session

The intervener began the session by describing the governing values that appeared in the first column of the map. For example, high respect on technical issues, low respect and trust on interpersonal issues, high commitment to hard work, high commitment to clients, high confidence that the firm could produce real value for clients, and high confidence that their technology was up to date. The directors did not have much difficulty in agreeing that these were their values. When asked if they could think of other governing values, several responded that they could not, but reserved the right to question or add to the list later.

Next came a series of questions about the causes of non-testing and blaming others. The intervener focused on the coerciveness of the system as well as on the directors' skillful behavior in bypassing and covering up. He did so because he wanted to make the point that the directors' actions were predictable from these factors and not from the untested attributions that they had made, such as saying that someone was power-oriented or competitive. Their attributions might have been valid, but the data did not directly support them at this time.

In acting this way, the intervener was illustrating actions and rules that he wanted the directors to learn. For example, whenever there are competing causal explanations, one should select those that are closest to the directly observable data. Also, one should strive to select causal explanations that require the smallest number of inferences from the available relatively directly observable data. Inferences about bypass and cover-up, for instance, can be tested by reference to tape recordings of actual behavior as well as by directors' reports of such incidents. However, inferences about being power hungry or competitive require inference processes that are much more complicated and difficult to test publicly on the basis of recordings.

It is more desirable to construct explanations, test predictions, design interventions, and make changes with the use of a simple inference structure, since the simpler the valid explanations, the more likely it is that tests can be crafted to be rigorous, intervention strategies to be reliable and complete, and the learning required for change to be produced with relative ease.

These rules have a further practical value. The shorter the chain of inferences from the directly observable data, the easier it will be for practitioners to test their hypotheses under conditions of everyday life. They can focus first on the actual behavior, then on the meaning of that behavior, and finally on their explanation of it. For example, focusing either on testing attributions or on determining whether they are testable is less likely to create the communication difficulties that arise when attributions of being power-hungry or having low self-esteem or a big ego are publicly defined and explained.

Inferences connected to what was said and done make it easier for the intervener to educate the clients. For example, when questions arise regarding alternative explanations, the intervener can make his or her views known and illustrate them while modeling the reasoning and the skills that he or she hopes to get the clients to consider. The intervener is not simply feeding back data but is beginning to create the conditions under which clients can choose, if they wish, to learn how to develop new causal framings of familiar issues.

Looking back, one can identify a trend in most groups whose members are genuinely interested in learning, a trend that occurred in this case as well. The conversations began with the directors' concerns about ideas and issues related to the intervener's theoretical positions. These centered on how skills can trap people, how it is possible to intend to be caring yet come across as uncaring, how untestable attributions lead to self-sealing consequences, and how these consequences become functional in the systems where the directors work.

The intervener emphasized that the directors were causally responsible for creating their defensive, limited-learning system and that this occurred even though they did not intend to hurt others or the organization as a whole.

Then the conversation shifted to an attempt by the directors to define the causes of their counterproductive actions, causes that were external and lay beyond their control. If they could find such causes, they seemed to think, they might be able to resolve their problematic situation without having to focus on such internal factors as their theories-in-use and personal responsibility. When the intervener suggested that these internal factors were crucial, he provoked a genuine confrontation of his views. Maybe what he assumed to be desirable was not? Maybe his argument was self-sealing? Who said that his normative position was correct? Maybe the directors were unable to change the factors that the intervener suggested should be changed? Could not the fault lie in the weaknesses of their technical knowledge? How about the siege mentality that developed because of client pressures?

The conversation entered its third phase when the directors returned to examining their personal responsibility. This led to the episode we examine below, in which the directors deal with their own internal politics. The episode begins with the CEO's candid reflections on how he builds coalitions and how he reacts to certain actions by the directors. This leads to a deeper analysis of what he and the other directors are doing to each other. The CEO describes the double bind he experiences. If he heeds many of the directors' complaints, he could conclude that the firm is in serious trouble and that he is responsible for solving the problem. If he does not heed the directors, he can be accused of being indifferent toward them or rejecting them. This leads other directors to explore their feelings about the CEO.

The conversation then turns to problems that plague most consulting organizations, including how to evaluate consultants' performance and how to allocate business leads fairly. This part of the conversation encourages the CEO to talk about what the directors do that leads him to feel victimized. The intervener adds that the directors might also feel victimized by the system they and the CEO have created. If the map is correct and the system is both self-sealing and anti-learning, then it could eventually lead everybody in the organization to feel victimized. The directors support this view.

CEO: I, too, want to discuss [internal politics and coalition building]. I plead guilty to coalition building for a substantive result in some cases. There is also coalition building where you truly want help aid discussion. But I have found that some people are inefficient participants. Even though I want genuine participation, I have learned to bias myself in favor of some of you more than others. Those that I choose do not give me a ten-hour answer, nor do I get the feeling that they are working out personal problems.

'JIM': But isn't that making attributions?

CEO: I agree. I would like to see all this changed. All I am doing is adding more data and asking that we put it on our agenda ... The whole currency is debased because, whenever someone is thanked, he goes around and makes speeches about how he saved someone's rear. Remember the motto we created for ourselves, 'Shut up and get back to work?' This could be interpreted as, 'Don't bother me with your problems; fix them yourselves'.

'DAVID': One reason that we are profitable is that we work hard. A work ethic driven out of fear is wrong. A work ethic driven out of a sense of teamwork, that you're achieving something, that's worth investing your life in, that's positive.

CEO: From my perspective, people working hard is not a problem because people love what they are doing. If we shut up and can't help or learn from each other, that would be a problem. How can we become the learning organization we say we want to become? How do we help clients become the learning organization that we say we can help them become?

Summary of the First Seminar

The topics discussed in the feedback session can be grouped into two broad categories. The first concerns the characteristics of the defensive, limited-learning organizational pattern and their interrelationships. It includes the following:

Undiscussable Attributions

- feeling plain ordinary fear of confrontation;
- thinking it is OK to have limited-learning systems and the politics that go with them;
- using a siege mentality to protect oneself;
- putting down clients;
- using technical knowledge to overawe;
- examining what it means to be a director;
- building coalitions, distancing by the CEO, and covering up both actions;
- describing the reciprocal distancing;
- haggling over who gets the credit;
- perceiving client leads to be allocated in accordance with secret rules and friendships; and
- needing to be strong by never asking for help.

Self-fulfilling and Self-sealing Consequences

1. The CEO feels double binds, bypasses, covers up, and becomes upset, all of which leads him to act like a 'blast furnace'. The other directors cover up their feelings; hence, these processes become undiscussable.
2. Directors create discussions that are not helpful and then assign responsibility to the CEO to take action. They condemn him for taking unilateral action.
3. Directors engage in distancing, which leads to more distancing and an increased likelihood that distancing is not discussable and hence is self-sealing.
4. Directors all feel victimized by a system they created.

System Paradoxes

1. Bypassing and covering up are functional with respect to the pattern that the directors have created and dysfunctional with respect to their vision of the firm.

2. Participation can lead to wasting a lot of time and can reduce the value of participation.

The second category includes topics that show the directors reflecting on the total pattern as well as on its implications.

Multiple Causality and Circularity

1. Individuals cover up, and the pattern rewards such actions. There is a circular relationship between individuals' responsibility for dysfunctional behavior and the patterns rewarding such behavior.
2. The tension is caused by wicked problems *and* by failure to deal with fear, embarrassment, or the sense of being threatened in the presence of these problems.
3. Directors make attributions about having nasty motives and about being power-oriented, competitive, and money-crazy.

Questions that Can be Used to Test Hypotheses

1. To what extent are dysfunctional consequences true for all organizations?
2. To what extent are directors able to change their theories-in-use and the ways they reason? To what extent do they wish to do so?
3. To what extent can directors assess their effectiveness as individuals and as a group?
4. To what extent can directors assess the intervener's normative views and values?

The directors provided many illustrations of the functioning of the whole pattern, along with its component parts and its possible impact on the organization's lower levels. The illustrations were, in many cases, enriched by explanatory comments. For example, a major portion of the time was spent talking about the impact of the CEO's actions upon individual directors and the group.

The feedback discussion also led members to describe how they felt victimized by the pattern. All of them, especially the CEO, reported continual double binds and explained how they came about.

As the members discussed the pattern, several things began to occur that provided important foundations for change. First, the directors confirmed that they made negative attributions about each other and that they did not test them or encourage others to do so. The apparent ease and candor with which they admitted their attributions provided evidence that the directors' intentions were not as nasty as the directors themselves evaluated them to be. Moreover, the directors appeared more capable of discussing undiscussable topics than they had originally thought they would be.

The very act of a thoughtful, spirited inquiry about the action map, in the context of a feedback session managed by an intervener, provided initial evidence that the over-protective features described in the map were valid but alterable. As a result the directors became optimistic about changing what they had feared was unchangeable. These changes in aspirations, we believe, came from the fact that the directors owned up to faults that were attributed to them in such a way as to disconfirm the further attribution that such faults were undiscussable. Moreover, when each director gave reasons for acting as he did, those reasons made sense to the others.

At the end of the session, all the directors expressed enthusiasm for the discussion that had occurred and a cautiously optimistic prognosis for change. There were at least two reasons why the optimism was cautious. First, many directors wondered what would happen after they left the room and especially what would happen when they returned to the pressures of everyday life. Second, as the intervener pointed out, in order for the optimism to become credible, new actions would have to develop and persist. In his opinion, the directors did not have the skills to produce the new actions even though they wanted to do so.

The intervener recommended a second seminar to examine the generic action strategies and the theories-in-use that produced them, to learn theories of action that could lead to more productive actions, to practice enacting these espoused theories so that they became a new theory-in-use, and to explore the organizational changes that the new theory-in-use could create. The directors agreed to hold this seminar.

The Second Seminar

Each director completed a left-hand/right-hand case as described in Chapter 4. Each case was discussed by the directors as a group. They acted as consultants to each other. All the cases illustrated features of Model I that we have described in several previous chapters. We will summarize how the cases and their discussion confirmed features of the action map presented earlier.

Action Strategies

The action strategies in the cases were consistent with Model I. For example, whenever the writers attempted to explain another person's intentions, the following actions were apparent:

- Negative attributions were made about the other's intentions and defensiveness.
- Attributions were not tested publicly.
- Negative evaluations were made about the other's performance.
- Evaluations were not tested publicly.
- The stated reason for avoiding testing was that the writer was showing concern for the other.

Cover-ups

The cases' left-hand columns contained the writers' attributions and evaluations of the CEO, other directors, and clients. They were not communicated to the other person in the conversation, yet these thoughts and feelings were crucial to the way each writer developed his strategies and produced his conversation.

Limited Learning

There was no reflection on or discussion of the critical issues that were being covered up. Moreover, each case showed that the writer protected himself, that the writer believed the CEO protected himself, and that underlying issues in the resource allocation system were never discussed.

Self-fulfilling and Self-sealing Processes

The case writers found serious faults with the allocation system and with the CEO's behavior. They entered into the dialogue doubting that the basic problems would be resolved. The way they crafted their conversations and censored them in order to cover up their thoughts and feelings made it likely that the problems identified in the cases would not be resolved by those conversations. Moreover, given the undiscussability of the left-hand columns and the Model I crafting of the conversation, it was unlikely that the parties would see that they were responsible for creating self-fulfilling processes as well as conditions under which these processes would not be discussed. Hence, their action strategies led to processes that sealed the dysfunctional processes, and these self-sealing processes were not discussed.

Embedded in this primarily Model I dialogue were signs of learning. For example, Jim raised doubts about the value of the case for learning, and several directors decried the use of 'bunny' cases because a norm was developing that such cases did not provide much food for learning. Individuals were beginning to make public their uncensored or left-hand-column thoughts, noting that before this seminar the thoughts would have remained censored. Bill appeared to look for an example of an attribution when he asked the others what case they thought would have been appropriate. Later, Jim began to use the concept of attribution, and also revealed his feelings about Bill's tone in the case and his anxiety that Bill was copping out.

Finally, Larry stated that the discussion was focused on 'ancient concerns'. This eventually led to a discussion of how the case might represent current issues. The session concluded with the directors evaluating it positively. They acknowledged that they had a long way to go to develop the competency that they desired. Indeed, several said that they now realized that this program was truly continuous and probably never-ending. They concluded by committing energy, time, and resources to continue the program.

Conducting Learning Experiments

In the next phase each director planned his own follow-up sessions. Each selected a problem that not only was important to him but that called for skills that, if he could develop them, would be applicable to many future problems. These sessions were also tape-recorded for research and educational purposes. The recordings were used to analyze the degree of progress the directors were making or the lack thereof, while the directors used the recordings to reflect on their learning and to further develop their skills.

The problems the directors selected represented crucial challenges to their skills and continued their learning. For example, two directors examined their mistrust of each other. A director questioned the underlying commitment of the CEO to his role in the firm. The directors examined the meaning of being an owner, and the CEO developed a new ownership plan that the directors approved. The directors then held a group evaluation of the CEO's performance. Two directors resolved the problem that each believed he was being undermined by the other.

An analysis of the tape recordings of these experiments indicates that the directors have continued to expand their range of competence to produce Model II conversations, although Model I has by no means disappeared.

The intervention was being expanded in several directions. First, sessions similar to the first ones in which the directors participated were offered throughout the organization. Second, concepts of Model II inquiry and learning were integrated into the education of senior consultants and case team managers. Third, a group of consultants was being prepared to become the internal change agents and educators for the firm. Finally, the intervention into the firm's client relationships has been expanded; for example, the firm is using action maps to describe important features of the behavioral worlds of the client organizations. The firm is also developing ways to produce maps that genuinely integrate behavioral features with technical features. Several directors have designed and implemented with senior clients change programs similar to the one they experienced. The left-hand/right-hand cases are routinely used to help clients diagnose and resolve double-loop problems. In some of the larger clients, change professionals and line managers are being educated in conducting these types of interventions.

CONCLUDING COMMENTS

In the literature already reviewed about normal science and the narrative mode, the writers suggest that there are important differences in their modes of thought. For example, Bruner (1986) and Tsoukas and Hatch (2001) suggest that these two modes are distinct because they are characterized by different logical organizations and are connected to different views of understanding and action.

The distinction being claimed is valid, I believe, as long as action and implementable validity are not taken seriously. For example, Bruner suggests that the central problem of the logico-scientific mode is to know the truth, whereas the central problem of the narrative mode is to endow experience with meaning. In all the examples we used (see Chapter 6) the central problem of all the participants was to realize that their theories-in-use produced meanings that contain inner contradictions. These inconsistencies were created skillfully and maintained by skilled unawareness. Their processes to endow experience with meaning did not survive robust tests of the claims of their validity. All their attempts to explain this away failed.

According to Bruner (1986), the strategy of the logico-scientific mode is empirical discovery guided by reasoned hypothesis. The narrative strategy is universal understanding grounded in personal experience. In all the examples, the participants produced their universal understanding through empirical discovery guided by reasoned hypothesis, namely, defensive reasoning. It took intervention that respected the logico-scientific methods of sound argument, tight analysis, reason, and proof to help them to see that their narrative methods of good stories, inspiring accounts, and intentions used defensive reasoning. Tests of validity were self-referential and closed to tests of even verisimilitude.

A key characteristic of the narrative approach of being meaning-centered and experimental turns out to be driven by theory that is categorical, general, and abstract—all characteristics of the logico-scientific mode.

Finally, we found that causality was a key feature of the action taken by the participants. In Chapter 6, the CEOs made many causal claims about Andy's resistance to learning. The left-hand/right-hand cases of the financial executives were full of causal claims about what they had to cover up in the name of caring and concern. In Chapter 2, the change professionals used theories-in-use to 'help' Tom that were abstract, decontextualized (from Tom's and the line managers' context), and ahistorical.

The interventions described in Chapters 6 and 7 combined features of the logico-scientific and narrative mode in ways that one would not expect from Bruner's characterization of the two modes. Bruner's analysis implies that each mode has its own consequences that should be respected. Our data suggests that there is a high degree of interdependency between the two modes, which surfaces, I believe, when interventions were created to help individuals produce effective action, especially those dealing with double-loop learning. It is interesting to note that Bruner conceives of these two modes as different modes of cognitive functioning, as two modes of thought, each providing distinctive ways of ordering experience, of constructing reality. I believe that this distinction makes sense when we limit the purposes of inquiry to be about understanding and explaining in the service of understanding and explaining, but is weak when our purpose is to understand and explain in the service of taking action, especially of the double-loop learning variety. Producing effective action requires many of the features of the logico-scientific and narrative modes combined. This deep interdependence surfaces when we strive for implementable validity about effective double-loop action.

Conclusion

Defensive reasoning by individuals, groups, intergroups, and organizations exists at all levels of organizations, and is manifest in activities ranging from planning, designing, formulating policies, and practices to the myriad of conversations related to managing organizations, to the execution of these activities. Defensive reasoning is omnipresent and powerful. It inhibits learning, especially when learning is most needed, when it is used to challenge existing routines and the status quo, and to innovate. Defensive reasoning is dangerous to organizational performance and effectiveness.

Defensive reasoning is doubly dangerous because it can overwhelm productive reasoning precisely when it is most needed. The reasons are as follows: (1) the tests for the validity of its claims are designedly weak, ambiguous, and easy to bypass; (2) the tests are intended to protect the actors more than to seek the truth about the claims being made; (3) the self-protective features are emphasized and sanctioned by the Model I theory-in-use and the organizational defensive routines; and (4) the self-protective features are so designed that defensive reasoning is strengthened by most of the current attempts to reduce it.

Defensive reasoning is triply dangerous because human beings become acculturated early in life to using it skillfully. Consequently, their sense of competence and their sense of confidence in their competence are threatened by attempts to expose its inherent counterproductive features such as skilled incompetence and skilled unawareness. Human beings become so attached to defensive reasoning that many see it as natural, realistic, and necessary. They are correct if the criteria of these features are the effective use of Model I and organizational defensive routines. The claim does not hold up if the counterproductive features of defensive reasoning are no longer taken for granted. The likelihood of this occurring is low because of the predisposition not to question and to reduce defensive reasoning in the first place.

Human beings have a choice to make. Will they back up defensive reasoning because it is protective of them and their organizations? Or will they choose to begin to dismantle the multi-level network of defensive reasoning activities in order to strengthen productive reasoning?

Research by scholars can, in principle, help human beings to make informed choices. In actuality, scholarly research appears to dodge this responsibility. It does so, I suggest, by using its own brand of defensive reasoning and by building norms in the scholarly community that support the limits placed on inquiry by the defensive reasoning mind-set. For example, in Chapter 5 I suggest several features of this mind-set. There is the norm that empirical research should focus on describing the universe 'as is' (that is, as constructed by scholars). Scholarly research does not focus on creating rare events, such as new universes, even though the results of such research can illuminate features of the 'as is' that surface when serious attempts are made to change the universe.

A complementary norm is the downgrading of normative research that is intended to produce prescriptive knowledge. It is often argued in defence of these norms that research that questions the status quo and seeks knowledge about new universes will arise in the normal course of the development of scholarly inquiry.

The analysis of the research cited in this book and others (Argyris 1980; 1993; 2000; Argyris and Schön 1996) questions the validity of this claim. A recent report written by scholars for the National Institute of Mental Health, cited in Chapter 5, also questions this claim.

The most powerful insights about the protective reasoning surrounding the norms that are protective of research surfaces when implementable validity is taken as seriously as internal and external validity. It is when attempts are made to implement the findings that we begin to realize that it is possible that knowledge, for example, about trust, can exhibit a high degree of external validity and a low degree of implementable validity.

I should like to turn to several recent scholarly studies conducted consistently with the best features of their respective disciplines to illustrate how the generalizability and applicability of the research is unintentionally limited precisely around testing the claims made by the researchers. First is an example that separates the cognitive from the emotional dimensions in ways that inhibit the listing of the authors' interesting model as well as the implementability of the advice (Gratton and Ghoshal 2002). The authors begin by recommending 'disciplined debate'. At the heart of disciplined debate is the continual testing of one's beliefs. The tests should go beyond confirmation toward falsification, focusing on questions such as: What data or evidence would they need to prove their assumptions to be wrong? What do they believe to be untrue that is actually true? This advice is consistent with productive reasoning. The authors also recommend that 'disciplined debate' be accompanied with 'intimate exchange' that helps to build empathy, mutual understanding, and truth. This is accomplished by re-personalizing the workplace so as to recognize that employees have feelings and emotions that affect their work.

In the case of disciplined debate, there is ample literature to inform the readers how to examine their beliefs systematically and logically. The authors begin with Socrates. It is possible to develop a relatively seamless connection between their advice and the actions required to implement it. However, the advice available in the literature on intimacy and feelings is more problematic. Seamlessness between thought and effective action is much more difficult to establish. For example, Charlotte Beers, then CEO of OgilvyOne, claims that, by having a dialogue around such questions as 'How do we feel about one another? Why can't we work together?', she was able to increase trust and group effectiveness. She also informs the readers that it took two years (plus changing some characters) to succeed.

Let us consider the readers who wish to implement the advice. The authors state that the way for them to begin to do so is to focus on the way they craft their conversations. In order for the readers to learn to craft their conversations more effectively, it would help them to be exposed to the conversations that occurred in the Beers' group. Unfortunately, Beers does not provide such descriptions. Similarly, Lord Browne (BP) is quoted as claiming that his relationships with Rodney Case (CEO) contained tough challenges but 'always in an appropriate way' (Gratton and Ghoshal 2002: 220). It would be helpful to have some illustrations of the conversations to help the reader understand what is appropriate and inappropriate.

Recall that the Intel CEO described his relationships with his immediate reports as being effective. Yet some of his immediate reports systematically withheld important information from him that would have partially falsified his claims. Also, recall the systematic cover-up and the cover-up of the cover-up by the CEOs in the Andy case, the financial and information technology executives, and the advanced MBA students. Perhaps the executives quoted by Gratton and Ghoshal (2002) did not experience such problems. It would have been helpful to include some conversations and analysis as to what happened.

It appears that the authors advise falsifications when crafting 'disciplined debate', but do not require the same level of analysis and proof for the 'intimate dialogue'. This may lead to the latter being considered 'soft' and the former 'hard'. Such a conclusion would be circular and self-sealing because the intimate conversations are subjected to softer analysis. I suggest that this is one fundamental reason for the deterioration of the practice of organizational development (Argyris 2004a).

Krogh, Ichijo, and Nonaka (2002) provide an interesting model of the creation of knowledge in organizations. The authors advise practitioners not to manage knowledge creation directly but to enable it. They suggest five knowledge enablers: instill a knowledge vision, manage conversations, mobilize knowledge activities, create the right context, and globalize local knowledge. Implementing these enablers, the authors advise, requires 'good human relationships' that purge the process of distrust and fear and break down personal and organizational barriers. A core feature of good human relationships is caring, because it produces increased awareness, mature personal relationships, learning, mutual trust, and active empathy, and encourages help and reliance on judgement consistent with productive inquiry. Caring, the authors claim, is produced through 'good conversations' that actively encourage participation, establish conversation etiquette, edit conversations appropriately, and foster innovative language.

Let us review this line of reasoning. The authors recommend the creation of good human relationships that purge mistrust, fear, and barriers to personal and organizational learning. They advise that at the core of producing these results is caring. But, as we have seen in Chapter 1, Model I caring is quite different from Model II caring. Moreover, as we have seen in Chapters 6 and 7, human beings are surprised that they do not produce good human relationships precisely when they believe they are doing so, and surprised by their skilled unawareness. They are more surprised by the skills they will have to learn and the behavioral systems they will have to create to implement Model II caring. Indeed, their early reaction is that Model II is, at best, romantic and unrealistic in the present-day world. The exploration of this reaction eventually leads them to realize that their fears are correct *and* that they are now faced with the choice of what are they going to do about it.

Habermas (1979) argues that human interaction presumes an 'ideal speech situation'. He suggests that linguistic communication involves four kinds of validity claims: that what is uttered is comprehensible, that the content of what is said is true, that the speaker is being truthful (the utterance is congruent with the speaker's intentions), and that the speech acts being performed are legitimate. If any of these validity claims are questioned,

Habermas calls for a 'discourse' in which the claims are examined and tested. The discourse is consistent with the features of the ideal speech situation. Habermas also argues that the ideal speech situation is the grounding for the ideas of rationality, freedom, and justice, as well as the idea of truth.

The ideal speech situation is consistent with the features of productive reasoning and Model II. Participants who choose to attend our seminars value the features of an ideal speech situation, but they do not have the skills to produce such a behavioral context and are unaware that this is the case. For example, the CEOs and Andy would claim that what they utter is comprehensible, that their content is true, that they are being truthful, and that their speech acts are legitimate. Yet they are unable to produce the discourse that Habermas recommends.

Dalton *et al.* (2002) conducted extensive and intensive empirical research on the ingredients of success for any global manager, studying 211 global and local managers over three years. Their fundamental assumption is that there is a relatively seamless connection between belief and action, and their causal theory is that this assumption holds if leaders have beliefs that they take to be valid and if the individuals already have the requisite skills. We have shown that there is a seamless connection between belief and action when the actions required are consistent with Model I. Some of the ingredients of effective leadership identified by the authors are consistent with Model I; but many are consistent with Model II.

Ellinger and Bostrom (2002) also assume that there is a causal relationship between managers' beliefs about facilitating learning and their implementation of the requisite actions. Data were collected on the beliefs of the managers. For example, managers reported that there was a distinction between managing and coaching (facilitating learning): managing was characterized as telling, judging, controlling, and directing, while coaching was about empowering, helping, developing, supporting, and removing obstacles. The latter features are consistent with Model II, the former with Model I.

The authors argue that coaching requires self-confidence. 'If you don't have confidence in yourself and your abilities, you are probably not going to feel like you can teach anybody anything' (Ellinger and Bostrom 2002: 161). The CEOs expressed great confidence in helping Andy, and also reported, as did the respondents of this study, that trust was critical in helping others.[1]

Weick and Sutcliffe (2002) have written a book intended primarily for practitioners focusing on the topic of assuring organizational high-performance, and especially on managing the unexpected. They focus their attention upon creating high-reliability organizations (HROs). One of their key recommendations is that a collective state of mindfulness should be created that produces an enhanced ability to discover and correct errors before they escalate into a crisis. The authors provide many case studies to show that errors are made because the organizational mind-set is primarily one of what they call mindlessness, not mindfulness.

A state of mindfulness is characterized by an ongoing scrutiny of existing expectations, by continuous refinement and differentiation based on new experiences, by willingness and capability to invent new expectations, by a more nuanced appreciation of context, and by the identification of new dimensions of context that improve foresight and current functioning.

Individuals seeking to learn mindfulness exhibit a preoccupation to learn from mistakes, a reluctance to simplify, a sensitivity to operations, and a commitment to resilience. The individuals also exhibit a preoccupation with updating, they accept the reality of ignorance, they focus on disconfirming and not simply confirming, and they respect uncertainty and the importance of the implicit.

What are the challenges faced if there is a desire to enhance mindfulness and to decrease mindlessness where the participants use Model I theory-in-use and where organizational defensive routines exist? It is possible to develop some relevant illustrations

---

[1] A similar gap between espoused theory and theory-in-use can be found in the study by Palus and Horth (2002).

by referring to the Andy Case and to the seminars where the left-hand/right-hand case methodology were used. For example, in the Andy Case the CEOs exhibited little of what the authors recommended to enhance mindfulness. They exhibited little updating, they did not accept the reality of ignorance, they focused primarily upon confirming and not disconfirming, and did so by using self-referential logic which assured self-fueling and self-sealing processes that inhibited their effectiveness.

In the left-hand/right-hand case material, we saw that the participants did not build capabilities to cope with error; indeed, they did not see themselves as making errors. Nor did they enhance mindfulness by focusing on cause rather than prevention. Their self-censorship strategies (left-hand columns) were primarily preventative. Many eased in to show concern. The easing-in strategy was interpreted as a 'lawyering, I-got-you' strategy. And the recipients dealt with their bewilderment and frustration by also easing in.

The advice offered by the authors to enhance mindfulness was violated continually by the participants in the cases that they wrote and in their actions in the classrooms where their behavior was tape-recorded. For example, the authors advise that individuals should carry their labels lightly in order to remain alert and flexible. The participants in our sessions would agree with this advice. But the CEOs, for example, would add that the data Andy produced were so overwhelmingly counterproductive that they had to carry their labels heavily. However, as we learned, the categories that they carried heavily they carried secretly (for example, CEOs never explored their private evaluations of Andy's actions). Also, the participants who wrote left- and right-hand cases crafted them with the intention of not making the others defensive, yet the opposite occurred.

The authors advise that executives should be suspicious of good news and seek out the bad news from Andy. The CEOs were given bad news by Andy. They ignored it publicly, but privately they interpreted it as evidence of Andy's defensiveness. There were many illustrations in the cases of writers being suspicious of good news (recall: 'like hell you enjoy meeting with me'). We could not find cases where the participants encouraged the expression of bad news, yet they believed that they did so. We reported similar findings in the left-hand/right-hand case studies that focused on business problems. There was little attempt to make underground cover-up strategies discussable. Indeed, striving to do so was seen as foolish, likely to be counterproductive, impractical, and at best romantic.

This should not be interpreted to mean that the authors are unaware of these underground organizational features. They provide many examples where defensive reasoning and defensive routines are important factors inhibiting mindfulness. For example, they point out that in most organizations information is used to justify decisions or positions already taken, preferences and effectiveness criteria are problematic, and conflicting decisions are often made in response to contests among interests for control over the organization. These features, the authors point out, are inconsistent with the pictures of organizations as rational, goal-driven, hierarchical designs that implement what strategists and planners set in motion.

Organizations are more like the first set of features than the second set of features described above. One reason is that the underground organizational features make it difficult to implement the rational designs embedded in the productive reasoning of managerial disciplines. This suggests an additional argument for developing theories of organizational leadership and design that take both productive and defensive reasoning into account. The theories should predict the counterproductive features of the interaction between the two mind-sets, and should also specify the nature of change programs that will lead to the strengthening of productive reasoning and the weakening of defensive reasoning.

Scholars could contribute significantly to this objective if they were to conduct research that provided knowledge about double-loop learning that had a high degree of implementable validity. Such research would open up new perspectives relevant to producing highly reliable organizations. For example, Weick and Sutcliffe (2002) define HROs as those that one can count upon not to fail in doing what is expected. They provide much thoughtful advice on how to enhance reliability with the use of essentially productive reasoning.

The underground organization with its defensive reasoning mind-set and generic syndrome inhibiting double-loop learning also meets the criterion of an HRO. The problem is that its high reliability is in the service of defensive protection that characterizes mindlessness and inhibits mindfulness. I believe that this dilemma will not be resolved without direct attention to reducing the defensive reasoning mind-set.

A recent front-page article in the *Financial Times* illustrates my belief. Roberts, Van Duyen, and Boyre (2002) quote the present CEO of ABB as saying: 'I really have to sort out what is wishful thinking and what is reality. I have to change the culture, especially to encourage more openness and transparency internally'.

Mr Dormann is the present chief executive officer and chairman of ABB. This is the same organization whose culture Percy Barnevik, a few years earlier, was recognized for transforming so that the organization faced reality and encouraged openness, transparency, initiative, and trust. The question arises: how did ABB lose all these features so quickly, given the laudatory description by many writers about the transformational change championed by Barnevik?

The 3M case also raises some interesting questions. What are the organizational processes that caused the deterioration of the 3M culture that produced innovativeness? How aware were the participants that the deterioration was occurring? If they were not, how do we explain their producing it? If they were aware, what caused the individuals to go along with it? Also, how did they cover up their collusion, and cover up the fact that they were not covering up?

Answers to these questions will help scholars to better understand and explain the nature of organizational culture and how it can be changed in ways that are effective and preserving. The answers will also help practitioners in disagreeing and producing cultural change. For example, they may be helped to see that the championing processes they use do communicate their commitment, but in ways that strengthen external commitment. External commitment may be necessary in large organizations; or it may be necessary at the outset, with internal commitment being generated as the program continues. External commitment is not necessarily wrong; what is counterproductive is for the top to champion the changes by championing internal commitment, and by making the inconsistency undiscussable.

Changes that genuinely transform organizations are not likely to persist as long as the defensive mind-set is not reduced. Similarly, if scholarship is to go beyond being the servant of the status quo, scholars will find it necessary to examine their defensive reasoning mind-set and the norms of their communities that support the mind-set. This will require research about double-loop learning that appears to produce knowledge that exhibits a high degree of implementable validity.

REFERENCES

Ackoff, R.L. (1999). *Re-creating the Organization*. New York: Oxford University Press.

Allison, G. (1971). *Essence of Decision–Explaining the Cuban Missile Crisis*. Boston, MA: Little, Brown.

Anderson, N., Herriot, R., and Hodgkinson, G. (2001). 'The Practitioner–Researcher Divide in Industrial Work and Organizational (IWO) Psychology: Where Are We Now and Where Do We Go from Here?' *Journal of Occupational and Organization Psychology*, 74: 391–411.

Argyris, C. (1957). *Personality and Organization*. New York: Harper and Bass.

—— (1962). *Interpersonal Competence and Organizational Effectiveness*. San Francisco, CA: Jossey-Bass.

—— (1964). *Integrating the Individual and the Organization*. New York: John Wiley.

—— (1965). *Organization and Innovation*. Homewood, IL: Irwin.

—— (1972). *The Applicability of Organizational Sociology*. Cambridge: Cambridge University Press.

—— (1976). 'Problems and New Directions for Industrial Psychology', in M. Dunnette (ed.), *Handbook of Industrial and Organizational Psychology*. Skokie, IL: Rand McNally.

—— (1980). *Inner Contradictions of Rigorous Research*. San Diego: Academic Press.

—— (1982). *Reasoning, Learning, and Action: Individual and Organizational*. San Francisco, CA: Jossey-Bass.

—— (1985). *Strategy, Change and Defensive Routines*. New York: Harper Business.

—— (1987). 'Reasoning, Action Strategies, and Defensive Routines: The Case of OD Practitioners', in R. Woodman and A. Pasmore (eds.), *Research in Organisational Change and Development*, i. Greenwich: JAI Press.

—— (1990a). *Overcoming Organizational Defenses*. Needham, MA: Allyn Bacon.

—— (1990b). 'Inappropriate Defenses Against the Monitoring of Organization Development Practice'. *Journal of Applied Behavioral Science*, 26/3: 299–312.

—— (1993). *Knowledge for Action: A Guide to Overcoming Barriers to Organizational Change*. San Francisco, CA: Jossey-Bass.

—— (1996). 'Unrecognized Defense of Scholars' Impact on Theory and Research'. *Organization Science*, 7/1: 77–85.

Argyris, C. (1997). 'Field Theory as a Basis for Scholarly Research-Consulting'. *Journal of Social Issues*, 53: 809–24.

—— (2000). *Flawed Advice and the Management Trap: How Managers Can Know When They're Getting Good Advice and When They're Not*. New York: Oxford University Press.

—— (2002). 'Double Loop Learning, Teaching, and Research'. *Academy of Management Learning and Education*, 1: 206–19.

Argyris, C. (2004a) 'On the Demise of Organizational Development', in D. Bradford and W. Burke (eds.), *The Demise of Organizational Development*

—— (forthcoming b). 'Implementing Core Competencies: A Theory of Action Perspective'.

—— and Kaplan, R. (1994). 'Implementing New Knowledge: The Use of Activity-Based Costing'. *Accounting Horizons*, 8/3: 83–105.

——, Putnam, R., and Smith, D. (1985). *Action Science*. San Francisco, CA: Jossey-Bass.

—— and Schön, D. (1974). *Theory in Practice*. San Francisco, CA: Jossey-Bass.

—— —— (1978). *Organizational Learning*. Reading, MA: Addison-Wesley.

—— —— (1994). *Theory in Practice: Increasing Professional Effectiveness*. San Francisco, CA: Jossey-Bass.

—— —— (1996). *Organizational Learning II*. Reading, MA: Addison-Wesley.

Avison, D. and Wood-Harper, A. (1990). *Multiview: An Exploration in Information Systems Development*. Oxford: Blackwell.

Axen, W., Fricke, T., and Thornton, A. (1991). 'The Microdemographic Community-Study Approach'. *Sociological Methods and Research*, 20/2: 187–217.

Bailey, F. (1988). *Humbuggery and Manipulation: The Art of Leadership*. Ithaca, NY: Cornell University Press.

Barber, J. (1977). *The Presidential Character*. Englewood Cliffs, NJ: Prentice-Hall.

Bardach, E. and Kagan, R. (1982). *Going by the Book*. Philadelphia: Temple University Press.

Barker, J. (1999). *The Discipline of Teamwork*. Thousand Oaks, CA: Sage.

Barker, R., Lewin, K., and Dembo, T. (1941). *Frustration and Regression: Studies in Child Welfare*. Iowa City: University of Iowa Press.

Barldoz, R., Kaaber, C., and Kraft, P. (2001). *The Critical Study of Work; Labor Technology and Global Production*. Philadelphia: Temple University Press.

Bazerman, M., Curhan, J., and Moore, D. (2000). 'The Death and Rebirth of Social Psychology and Negotiation', in G. Fletcher and M. Clark (eds.), *Blackwell Handbook of Social Psychology: Interpersonal Processes*. Oxford: Blackwell.

Beatty, C. and Schachter, H. (2002). *Employee Ownership*. New York: John Wiley.

Beer, M. (2002). *Building Organizational Fitness in the 21ˢᵗ Century*. Boston, MA: Harvard Business School (Working Paper No. 02-044).

Bennsaou, M. and Earl, M. (1998). 'The Right Mindset for Managing Information Technology'. *Harvard Business Review*, Sept.–Oct.: 119–28.

Bentley, T. (1998). *Managing Information: Avoiding Overload*. London: Chartered Institute of Management Accountants.

Berliner, J. (1957). *Factory and Manager in the U.S.S.R.* Cambridge, MA: Harvard University Press.

Bloomfield, B. and Vurdubakis, T. (1997). 'Visions of Organizational Vision: The Representational Practices of Information Systems Development'. *Accounting, Organizations and Society*, 22: 639–68.

Boje, D. (2001). *Narrative Methods for Organizational and Communication Research.* London: Sage Publications.

Bolman, L. and Deal, T. (1991). *Reframing Organizations: Artistry, Choice, and Leadership.* San Francisco, CA: Jossey-Bass.

Bruner, J. (1986). *Actual Minds, Possible Worlds.* Cambridge, MA: Harvard University Press.

Brunsson, N. (1989). *The Organization of Hypocrisy.* New York: John Wiley.

Burawoy, M. (2001). 'Dwelling in Capitalism; Traveling through Socialism', in R. Baldoz, C. Kaeber, and P. Kraft (eds.), *The Critical Study of Work: Labor Technology and Global Production.* Philadelphia: Temple University Press.

Burgelman, R. (1994). 'Fading Memories: A Process Theory of Strategic Business Exit in Dynamic Environments'. *Administrative Sciences Quarterly*, 39: 24–56.

—— (2002a). *Strategy is Destiny.* New York: The Free Press.

—— (2002b). 'Strategy as Vector and the Inertia of Coevolutionary Lock-In'. *Administrative Science Quarterly*, 47: 325–57.

Burns, J.(1978). *Leadership.* New York: HarperCollins.

Burns, T. and Stalker, G. (1961). *The Management of Innovation.* London: Tavistock.

Cameron, J. and Pierce, W. (2001). *Rewards & Intrinsic Motivation: Resolving the Controversy.* Westport, CT: Bergen & Garvey.

Campbell, D. and Stanley, J. (1963). *Experimental and Quasi-experimental Design for Research.* Skokie, IL: Rand-McNally.

Carse, James (1986). *Finite and Infinite Games.* New York: Ballantine Books.

Case, P. (1999). 'Remember Re-Engineering: The Rhetorical Appeal of A Managerial Salvation Device'. *Journal of Management Studies*, 38: 419–42.

Charan, R. and Useem, J. (2002). 'Why Companies Fail'. *Fortune*, 27 May: 50–62.

Christensen, C. and Overdorf, M. (2000). 'Meeting the Challenge of Descriptive Change'. *Harvard Business Review*, March–April: 66–76.

Churchland, P. (2000). *The Engine of Reason, the Seat of the Soul.* Cambridge, MA: MIT Press.

Ciampa, D. and Watkins, M. (1999). *Right From The Start.* Cambridge, MA: Harvard Business School Press.

Ciborra, C. (2001). *From Control to Drift.* Oxford: Oxford University Press.

—— (2002). *The Labyrinths of Information.* Oxford: Oxford University Press.

Cyert, R. and March, J. (1963). *A Behavioral Theory of the Firm.* Englewood Cliffs, NJ: Prentice-Hall.

Czarniawska, B. (1999). *Writing Management.* New York: Oxford University Press.

Daft, R. (1983). *Organization Theory and Design.* St Paul, MN: West.

Dalton, M., Ernst, C., Deal, J., and Leslie, J. (2002). *Success for the New Global Manager.* San Francisco, CA: Jossey-Bass.

Damasio, A. (1994). *Descartes' Error*. New York: G. P. Putnam's Sons.

Danziger, J. and Kraemer, K. (1986). *People and Computers*. New York: Columbia University Press.

Davenport, T. and Prusak, L. (1998). *Working Knowledge*. Boston, MA: Harvard Business School Press.

Davis, G., Lee, A., Nickles, K., Chatterjee, S., Hartung, R., and Wu, Y. (1992). 'Diagnosis of an Information Systems Failure'. *Information and Management*, 23: 293–312.

De Charm, R. (1968). *Personal Causation*. New York: Academic Press.

—— (1976). *Embracing Motivation*. New York: Irvington.

De Sousa, R. (1991). *Origins of the Modern Mind*. Cambridge, MA: Harvard University Press.

Doherty, N. and King, M. (1998). 'The Importance of Organizational Issues in Systems Development'. *Information Technology and People*, 11/2: 104–23.

Donaldson, L. (1985). *In Defence of Organization Theory*. Cambridge: Cambridge University Press.

Drejer, A. (2002). *Strategic Management and Core Competencies*. Westport, CT: Quorum Books.

Dror, J. (2002). *The Capacity to Govern*. London: Frank Cass.

Drory, A. and Romm, T. (1990). 'The Definition of Organizational Politics: A Review'. *Human Relations*, 43: 1133–54.

Dyer, G. Jr. and Wilkins, A. (1991). 'Better Stories, Not Better Constructs, to Generate Better Theory: A Rejoinder to Eisenhardt'. *Academy of Management Review*, 16: 613–9.

Economist (2002). 'How About Now'. 2 February: 3–20.

Edelman, M. (1988). *Constructing the Political Spectacle*. Chicago, IL: University of Chicago Press.

Edmondson, A. (1996) 'Three Faces of Eden: The Persistence of Competing Theories and Multiple Diagnoses in Organizational Intervention Research'. *Human Relations*, 49: 571–95.

Eisenhardt, K. (1989). 'Building Theories from Case Study Research'. *Academy of Management Review*, 14: 532–50.

—— and Bourgois, L., II (1988). 'Politics of Strategic Decision Making in High-Velocity Environments: Toward a Mid-range Theory'. *Academy of Management Journal*, 4: 737–70.

Ellinger, A. and Bostrom, R. (2002). 'An Examination of Managers' Beliefs About Their Roles as Facilitators of Learning'. *Journal for Managerial Learning*, 33/2: 147–80.

Etheredge, L. (1985). *Can Governments Learn?* Elmsford, NY: Pergamon Press.

Fincham, R. (2002). 'Narratives of Success and Failure in Systems Development'. *British Journal of Management*, 13: 1–14.

Flyvbjerg, B. (2001). *Making Social Science Matter*. Cambridge: Cambridge University Press.

Frese, M., Kring, W., Soose, A., and Zempel, J. (1996). 'Personal Initiative at Work: Differences Between East and West Germany'. *Academy of Management Journal*, 39/1: 37–63.

Friedman, B. (1997). *Human Values and the Design of Computer Technology*. Stanford, CA: CSLT Publications.

Friedman, V., Lipshitz, R., and Overmeer, W. (2001). 'Creating Conditions For Organizational Learning', in J. Dierkes, J. Child, and I. Nonaka (eds.), *Handbook of Organizational Learning*. London: Sage.

Gabriel, Y. (2000). *Storytelling in Organizations*. Oxford: Oxford University Press.

Galliers, R. and Baets, W. (1998). *Information Technology and Organizational Transformation*. Chichester: John Wiley & Sons.

Gardner, J. (1990). *On Leadership*. New York: Free Press.

Garvin, D. (1995). 'Leveraged Process for Strategic Advantage'. *Harvard Business Review*, Sept.–Oct.: 77–90.

George, A. (1972). 'The Case of Multiple Advocacy in Making Foreign Policy'. *American Political Science Review*, 67: 751–85.

Gibson, J. and Tesone, D. (2001). 'Management Fads' Emergence, Evolution, and Implications for Managers'. *Executive*, 15/4: 122–33.

Giddens, A. (1976). *New Rules of Sociological Method*. London: Hutchinson.

Gill, J. and Johnson, P. (1991). *Research Methods for Managers*. London: Chapman.

Goggin, W. (1974). 'How The Multi-Dimensional Structure Works at Dow Corning'. *Harvard Business Review*, 52: 54–65.

Gold, J., Holman, D., and Thorpe, R. (2002). 'The Role of Argument Analysis and Storytelling in Facilitating Critical Thinking'. *Management Learning*, 33: 371–87.

Golding, D. (1991). 'Some Everyday Rituals in Management Control'. *Journal of Management Studies*, 28: 569–84.

Gouldner, A. (ed.) (1950). *Studies in Leadership*. New York: Harper.

Gratton, L. and Ghoshal, S. (2002). 'Improving the Quality of Conversations'. *Organizational Dynamics*, 31: 209–23.

Grint, K. (2000). *The Art of Leadership*. Oxford: Oxford University Press.

——and Case, P. (1998). 'The Violent Rhetoric of Re-Engineering: Management Consultancy on the Offensive'. *Journal of Management Studies*, 35: 557–78.

Habermas, J. (1972). *Knowledge and Human Interest*. London: Heinemann

——(1979). *Communication and Evaluation of Society*. Boston, MA: Beacon Press.

Hackman, J. (1987). 'The Design of Work Teams', in J. Lorsch (ed.), *Handbook of Organizational Behavior*. Englewood Cliffs, NJ: Prentice-Hall.

——(ed.) (1989). *Groups that Work (And Those that Don't): Creating Conditions for Effective Teamwork*. San Francisco, CA: Jossey-Bass.

Halal, W. (1986). *The New Capitalism*. New York: John Wiley.

Halperin, M. (1974). *Bureaucratic Politics and Foreign Policy*. Washington, DC: Brookings Institution.

Hassard, J. (1991). 'Multiple Paradigms and Organizational Analysis: A Case Study'. *Organization Studies*, 12: 275–99.

Hatchuel, A. (2001). 'The Two Pillars of Management Research'. *British Journal of Management*, 12: 41–8.

Heller, F. (1998). 'Influence at Work: A 25-year Program of Research'. *Human Relations*, 51: 1425.

Heller, F. Pusic, G., Strauss, G., and Wilpert, B. (1998). *Organizational Participation: Myth and Reality*. Oxford: Oxford University Press.

Hedberg, B., Dahlgren, G., Hansson, J., and Olve, N. (1997). *Virtual Organizations and Beyond*. Chichester: John Wiley & Sons.

Holland, J. (1993). 'Complex Adaptive Systems', in N. Metropolis and G. Rota (eds.), *A New Era in Computation*. Cambridge, MA: MIT Press.

Hollingshead, G. and Mickavilovs, S. (2001). 'Blockbusters or Bridge-Builders?' *Management Learning*, 32: 419–36.

Introna, L. and Whitley, E. (1997). 'Against Method-ism'. *Information Technology and People*, 10: 31–45.

Jackson, N. and Carter, P. (1991). 'In Defense of Paradigm Incommensurability'. *Organization Studies*, 12/1: 109–27.

Jackson, T. (1997). *Inside Intel*. New York: Dutton Books.

Janis, I. (1972). *Victims of Group Think*. Boston, MA: Houghton Mifflin.

——(1989). *Crucial Decisions: Leadership in Policymaking and Crisis Management*. New York: Free Press.

Jensen, M. (2000). *A Theory of the Firm: Governance, Residual Claims, and Organizational Forms*. Cambridge, MA: Harvard University Press.

Johnson, D. (1993). 'Psychology in Washington: Measurement to Improve Scientific Productivity: A Reflection on the Brown Report'. *Psychological Science*, 4/2: 67–9.

Kahn, R., Wolfe, D., Quinn, R. Snoek, J., and Rosenthal, R. (1964). *Organizational Stress: Studies in Role Conflict and Ambiguity*. New York: John Wiley.

Katz, D. and Kahn, R. (1966). *The Social Psychology of Organizations*. New York: John Wiley.

Katzenback, J. and the RCL Team (1995). *Real Change Leaders*. New York: Random House.

Kaufman, H. (1981). *The Administrative Behavior of Bureau Chiefs*. Washington, DC: Brookings Institution.

——(1977). *Red Tape*. Washington, DC: Brookings Institution.

Kelemen, M. and Bansal, P. (2002). 'The Conventions of Management Research and Their Relevance to Management Practice'. *British Journal of Management*, 13/2: 97–108.

Kellerman, B. (ed.) 1984). *Leadership: Multidisciplinary Perspectives*. Englewood Cliffs, NJ: Prentice-Hall.

Kipping, M. and Engwall, G. (eds.) (2002). *Management Consulting*. Oxford: Oxford University Press.

Krogh, G., Ichijo, K., and Nonaka, I. (2002). *Enabling Knowledge Creation*. Oxford: Oxford University Press.

Kubie, L. (1958). *Neurotic Distortions of the Creative Process*. Lawrence: University of Kansas Press.

Kumar, P. and Ghadially, R. (1989). 'Organizational Politics and its Effects on Members of Organizations'. *Human Relations*, 4: 305–14.

Lammers, C. (1974). 'Self Management and Participation: Two Concepts of Decentralization in Organizations'. *Organization and Administrative Science*, 5/4: 17–33.

Landon, K. and Landon, J. (1998). *Management Information Systems*. Upper Saddle River, NJ: Prentice-Hall.

Lawrence, P. and Lorsch, J. (1967). *Organization and Environment: Managing Differentiation and Integration.* Boston, MA: Harvard Business School Press.

—— and Vlacoutsicos, C. (1990). *Behind the Factory Walls.* Boston, MA: Harvard Business School Press.

Leetis, N. (1985). *Soviet Style in Management.* New York: Crane Russak.

Levitt, B. and March, J. (1988). 'Organizational Learning'. *Annual Review of Sociology,* 14: 319–40.

Lewin, K. (1935). *A Dynamic Theory of Personality.* New York: McGraw-Hill.

—— (1951). 'Field Theory and Learning', in D. Cartwright (ed.), *Field Theory and Social Science: Selected Papers by Kurt Lewin.* New York: Harper and Brothers.

—— Lippitt, R., and Escalona, S. (1940). *Studies in Topological and Vector Psychology.* Iowa City: University of Iowa Press.

Lincoln, N., Travers, C., Ackers, P., and Wilkinson, A. (2002). 'The Meaning of Empowerment: The Interdisciplinary Etymology of a New Management Concept'. *International Journal of Management Reviews,* 4/3: 271–90.

Lipshitz, R. (2000). 'Chic, Mystique, and Misconception'. *Journal of Applied Behavioral Science,* 36: 456–73.

—— and Popper, M. (2000). 'Organizational Learning in a Hospital'. *Journal of Applied Behavioral Science,* 36: 345–61.

Lucas, H. (1981). *Implementation: The Key to Successful Information Systems.* New York: Columbia University Press.

Lucas, Jr., H., Ginzberg, M., and Schultz, R. (1990). *Information Systems Implementation.* Norwood, NJ: Ablex Publishing.

Lynn, L. and Whitman, D. deF. (1981). *The President as Policy Maker: Jimmy Carter and Welfare Reform.* Philadelphia: Temple University Press.

McFarland, A. (1969). *Power and Leadership in Pluralistic Systems.* Stanford, CA: Stanford University Press.

McGrath, J., Martin, J., and Kukla, R. (1982). *Judgment Calls in Research.* Newbury Park, CA: Sage.

Malone, T. (1997). 'Is Empowerment Just a Fad? Control, Decision Making and Information Technology'. *Sloan Management Review,* 28/2: 23–35.

——, Crowston, K., Lee, J., Pentaland, B., Dellarocas, C., Wyner, G., Quimby, J., Osborne, C., and Bernstein, A. (1997). *Tools for Inventing Organizations: Toward a Handbook of Organizational Processes.* Cambridge, MA:. Center for Coordination Science, Massachusetts Institute of Technology (Report No. 198).

March, J. (1981). 'Decision Making Perspective', in A. Van De Ven and W. Joyce (eds.), *Perspectives on Organizational Design and Behavior.* New York: John Wiley & Sons.

—— (1988). *Decisions and Organizations.* Oxford: Blackwell.

Martin, R. (1990). 'Deconstructing Organizational Taboos: The Suppression of Gender Conflict in Organizations'. *Organization Science,* 1: 339–59.

—— (2002). *The Responsibility Virus.* New York: Basic Books.

Mayes, Allen (1983). 'Toward a Definition of Organizational Politics', in R. Allen and L. Porter (eds.), *Organizational Influence Processes.* Glenview, IL: Scott, Foresman.

Mead, M. (1951). *Soviet Attitudes Toward Authority: An Interdisciplinary Approach to Problems of Soviet Character*. New York: McGraw-Hill.

Mendelson, H. and Ziegler, J. (1999). *Survival of the Smartest*. New York: John Wiley.

Mills, O. (2002). *Buy, Lie, and Sell High: How Investors Lost on Enron and the Internal Bubble*. Upper Saddle River, NJ: Financial Times, Prentice-Hall.

Mills, P. and Ungson, G. (2003). 'Reassessing the Limits of Structural Empowerment: Organizational Constitution and Trust as Controls'. *Academy of Management Review*, 28: 143–53.

Miner, A. and Meziac, S. (1996). 'Ugly Ducking No More: Pasts and Futures of Organizational Learning Research'. *Organization Science*, 7/1: 88–99.

Morgan, G. (1983). *Beyond Method*. Newbury Park, CA: Sage.

——and Smircich, L. (1980). 'The Case for Qualitative Research'. *Academy of Management Review*, 5: 491–500.

Morse J. and Lorsch, J. (1970). 'Beyond Theory Y'. *Harvard Business Review*, May–June: 61–8.

Nardi, B. and O'Day, V. (1999). *Information Ecologies*. Cambridge, MA: MIT Press.

Nass, C., Moon, Y., Morkes, J., Kim, E-Y., and Fogg, B. (1997). 'Computers are Social Actors: A Review of Current Research', in B. Friedman (ed.), *Moral and Ethical Issues in Human-Computer Interaction*. Stanford, CA: CSLI Press.

Nelson, R. and Winter, S. (1982). *An Evolutionary Theory of Economic Change*. Cambridge, MA: The Belknap Press of Harvard University Press.

Neustadt, R. and May, E. (1986). *Thinking in Time*. New York: Free Press.

Nielson, P. and Nørjberg, J. (2001). 'Assessing Software Processes: Low Maturity or Sensible Practice'. *Scandinavian Journal of Information Systems*, 13: 51–67.

NIMH (National Institute of Mental Health Study) (2001). *Translating Behavioral Science into Action* (Report of the National Advisory Mental Health Council's Behavioral Science Workgroup). Bethesda, MD: National Institutes of Health (Publication No. 00-4699).

Nonaka, I., Reinmoller, P., and Toyama, R. (2001). 'Integrated Information Technology Systems for Knowledge Creation', in M. Dierkes *et al.* (eds.), *Organizational Learning and Knowledge*. New York: Oxford University Press.

——and Takeuchi, H. (1995). *The Knowledge Creating Company*. New York: Oxford University Press.

——, Toyama, R., and Byosière, P. (2001). 'A Theory of Organizational Knowledge Creation: Understanding the Dynamic Process of Creating Knowledge', in M. Dierkes *et al.* (eds.), *Organizational Learning and Knowledge*. New York: Oxford University Press.

Norman, D. (1998). *The Invisible Computer*. Cambridge, MA: MIT Press.

Nutt, R. (2002). *Why Decisions Fail*. San Francisco, CA: Berritt-Koehler Publishers.

O'Dell, C. and Grayson, C. (1998). *If Only We Knew What We Know*. New York: Free Press.

Paige, G. (1977). *The Scientific Study of Political Leadership*. New York: Free Press.

Palus, C. and Horth, D. (2002). *The Leader's Edge*. San Francisco, CA: Jossey-Bass.

Parker, C. (2002). *The Open Corporation*. Cambridge: Cambridge University Press.

Perrow, C. (1984). *Normal Accidents: Living with High Risk Technologies*. New York: Basic Books.

Perry, B. (1984). *Enfield: A High Performance System*. Bedford, MA: Digital Educational Services Development and Publishing.

Peters, M. and Robinson, V. (1984). 'The Origins and Status of Action Research'. *Journal of Applied Behavioral Science*, 20/2: 113–24.

Pettigrew, A. (2001). 'Management Research After Modernism'. *British Journal of Management*, 12: 61–71.

Popper, K. (1959). *The Logic of Scientific Inquiry*. New York: Basic Books.

Popper, M. and Lipshitz, R. (2000). 'Organizational Learning: Mechanisms, Culture, and Feasibility'. *Management Learning*, 31/2: 181–96.

Porter, M. (1980). *Competitive Strategy*. New York: Free Press.

Presidential Commission (1986). *On the Space Shuttle Challenger Accident*. Washington, DC: US Government Printing Office.

Puffer, S., McCarthy, D., and Nwumov, A. (2000). *The Russian Capitalist Experiment: From State-Owned Organizations to Entrepreneurships*. Cheltenham: Edward Elgar.

Rentsch, J. (1990). 'Climate and Culture: Interaction and Qualitative Differences in Organizational Meanings'. *Journal of Applied Psychology*, 75: 668–81.

Roberts, D., Van Duyn, A., and Bower, C. (2002). 'ABB on Verge of Collapse Amid Growing Asbestos Woes'. *Financial Times*. 23 October: 1.

Robertson, I., Callinan, M., and Bartram, D. (eds.) (2002). *Organizational Effectiveness: The Role of Psychology*. Chichester: John Wiley.

Robinson, V. (1993). *Problem-Based Methodology*. Oxford: Pergamon Press.

Rockart, J., Earl, M., and Ross, W. (1996). 'Eight Imperatives for the New IT Organization'. *Sloan Management Review*, 38/1: 43–53.

Rosen, M. (1991). 'Coming to Terms with the Field: Understanding and Doing Organizational Ethnography'. *Journal of Management Studies*, 28/1: 1–24.

Ross, J. and Staw, B. (1986). 'Expo 86: An Escalation Prototype'. *Administrative Science Quarterly*, 31: 274–97.

Roth, G. and Kleiner, A. (2000). *Car Launch*. New York: Oxford University Press.

Salter, M. (2003). *Innovation Corrupted: The Rise and Fall of Enron*. Cambridge, MA: Harvard Business School.

Sander, K. (1990). 'Organizational Development as a Political Process', in F. Massarek (ed.), *Advances in Organizational Development*, i. Norwood, NJ: Ablex.

Sayles, L. (1989). *Leadership*. New York: McGraw-Hill.

Schein, E. (1987a). *The Clinical Perspective in Fieldwork*. Newbury Park, CA: Sage.

—— (1987b). *Process Consultation*, ii. Reading, MA: Addison-Wesley.

Schön, D. (1967). *Technology and Change: The New Heraclitus*. New York: Delacorte Press.

—— (1983). *The Reflective Practitioner*. New York: Basic Books.

Scott, W. (1981). *Organizations: Rational, Natural, and Open Systems*. Englewood Cliffs, NJ: Prentice-Hall.

Senge P. (1990). *The Fifth Discipline*. New York: Doubleday.

Sennett, R. (1998). *The Corrosion of Character*. New York: W. W. Norton.

Sennett, R. and Cobb, J. (1972). *The Hidden Injuries of Class*. New York: W.W. Norton.

Simon, H. (1969). *The Science of the Artificial*. Cambridge, MA: MIT Press.

Sköldberg, K. (2002). *The Poetic Logic of Administration: Styles and Changes of Style in the Art of Organizing*. London, New York: Routledge.

Sproull, L. and Kiesler, S. (1991). *Connections*. Cambridge, MA: MIT Press.

Starkey, K. and Madan, P. (2001). 'Budging the Relevance Gap: Aligning Stakeholders in the Future of Management Research'. *British Journal of Management*, 12: 3–27.

Stockman, David A. (1986a). *The Triumph of Politics: How the Reagan Revolution Faded*. New York: Harper and Row.

—— (1986b). 'The Disillusionment of David Stockman'. *Frontline*. 20 April (transcript from PBS station WGBH, Boston).

Teece, D. (1998). 'Capturing Value from Knowledge Assets: The New Economy, Markets for Know-How and Intangible Assets'. *California Management Review*, 40/3: 55–78.

Tsoukas, H. and Hatch, M. (2001). 'Complex Thinking, Complex Practice: The Case for A Narrative Approach to Organizational Complexity'. *Human Relations*, 54: 979–1013.

Van de Ven, A. and Polley, D. (1992). 'Learning While Innovating'. *Organizational Science*, 3/1: 92–115.

Van der Heijden, J., with Bradfield, R., Burt, G., Cairne, G., and Wright, G. (2002). *The Sixth Sense: Accelerating Organizational Learning with Scenarios*. New York: John Wiley.

Van Maanen, J. (1982). 'Introduction', in Van Maanen et al. (eds.), *Varieties of Qualitative Research*. Newbury Park, CA: Sage.

Von Krogh, G., Ichijo, K., and Nonaka, I. (2000). *Enabling Knowledge Creation*. New York: Oxford University Press.

Wall Street Journal (2002). 23 April: 1.

Weick, K. (2001). 'Gapping the Relevance Bridge: Fashions Meet Fundamentals in Management Research'. *British Journal of Management*, 12: 70–6.

—— and Sutcliffe, K. (2002). *Managing the Unexpected*. San Francisco, CA: Jossey-Bass.

Wheelan, S., Pepitone, E., and Abt, V. (1990). *Advances in Field Theory*. Newbury Park, CA: Sage.

White, R. (1956). 'Motivation Reconsidered: The Concept of Competence'. *Psychological Review*, 66: 297–333.

Whyte, W. (1991). *Social Theory for Action: How Individuals and Organizations Learn to Change*. Newbury Park, CA: Sage.

Willmott, H. (1997). 'Management and Organization Studies as Science'. *Organization*, 4: 309–44.

Wilson, J. (1989). *Bureaucracy*. New York: Basic Books.

Wrong, D. (1961). 'The Over-Socialized Conception of Men in Modern Sociology'. *American Sociological Review*, 26: 183–93.

INDEX